TOM LANDRY

MAN OF CHARACTER

DONNIE SNYDER

WITH

KEN HORTON

D1371969

TOM LANDRY: MAN OF CHARACTER

Cross Training Publishing
P.O. Box 1874
Kearney, NE 68848
(308) 293-3891

Copyright © 2009 by Donnie Snyder and Ken Horton

ISBN: 978-0-9821652-7-0

This book is manufactured in the United States of America.

This book is dedicated to Coach Tom Landry
"A life lived with character"

and

To Jim Myers and every other coach in America who strives to
use their platform to develop Christian character
in the lives of the athletes and people they influence.

Acknowledgements

I would like to express my appreciation to Ken Horton for providing the Biblical examples of character at the end of each chapter and for his belief in the Fellowship of Christian Athletes. Additionally, my heartfelt thanks go to Bob Lilly, Scott Murray, Dan Reeves, Kyle Rote, Jr. Grant Teaff and Dal Shealy for their contributions to this book.

Contents

Foreword
Dan Reeves
Former Player and Coach Dallas Cowboys
Head Coach Denver Broncos,
New York Giants and Atlanta Falcons

Other than my mother and father, the people that had the greatest influence on my life, were my football coaches. In high school it was Jimmy Hightower, in college it was Marvin Bess and in the NFL it was Coach Tom Landry.

Coach Landry felt that coaches and players could help instill the character in young people that is so desperately needed today. I was fortunate to spend sixteen years of my life watching and learning from a man who was not only one of the greatest football coaches of all time, but was more importantly one of the greatest men of character in America.

My first five years playing for the Dallas Cowboys under Coach Landry, we were labeled as "next year's champion." We lost the NFL Championship game to the Green Bay Packers in 1966 and 1967 for the right to go to Super Bowls I and II. We lost to the Cleveland Browns in 1968 and 1969 for the NFL Eastern Division Championship. These were extremely difficult losses and Coach Landry's' great character always came through as he handled the disappointment with great "class" and was an example for us all.

After the 1969 season, Coach Landry asked me to be a

player-coach and for the next three years I served in that capacity. From that position I was able to see a side of Coach Landry that you simply do not see as a player. Working with him on a daily basis as a coach, I got to see his incredible character and integrity in action every day.

We finally went to the Super Bowl in 1970, only to come up short once again losing to the Baltimore Colts by a last second field goal. Coach Landry never gave up and finally we beat the Miami Dolphins in the 1972 Super Bowl to become world champions. The entire team and staff were all so excited, but for me one of the greatest thrills was to see Coach Landry carried off the field by his players. He was our leader who had shown so much character throughout all of those tough losses that had ended so many of our seasons in the past.

My last eight years with the Dallas Cowboys was as a full-time assistant coach giving me further insight on why Coach Landry was so successful. He was one of the most organized people you have ever seen and highly competitive. In fact, after the season was over, he would not play golf with Mike Ditka and me unless he had a couple of lessons and hit balls for a couple weeks. Preparation was just simply a part of his character and a very good life principle for us all.

The thing I admired far and above anything else about Coach Landry was how he handled his Christian faith and his family. His daily walk with our Lord was truly amazing. To repeat an old cliché, he not only "talked the talk," more importantly he "walked the walk." He simply was a great example to us all about what a Christian man should be. We all admired how much he loved his family and showed what they meant to him.

One of his greatest influences on me was how much he demonstrated his love for his beautiful wife, Alicia. I always said they were the best looking couple in the NFL and Alicia traveled with us on road trips. The example that he set as a man loving his wife made a huge positive impact on every coach and every player. Coach Landry showed us how a man was intended to treat his wife. It influenced me so much, that I began to have my wife Pam, join us in the same manner when I became Head Coach of the Denver Broncos and carried that example to New York with the Giants and to Atlanta with the Falcons.

Coach Landry's character was lived out in so many ways. Coach Landry believed that you could demonstrate character by how you treated people who were not in a position to do anything for you. He was genuinely nice to everyone.

When I became Head Coach of the Denver Broncos in 1981, Coach Landry gave me the two greatest pieces of advice that I continue to use today. He said first, "be yourself," because people will quickly pick up on it if you are being a phony. Second, he said "always tell the truth, because if you don't you can't ever remember what you have said."

Like many, my life was forever changed by the character of the "Man in the Hat." How fortunate I was to play for, work for and be friends with one of the greatest men of character our country has ever known, "Tom Landry–Man of Character."

*"First become a winner in life.
Then it's easier to become a winner on the field."*

- Tom Landry

Introduction

**Character is a difficult thing to describe,
but once you have seen it, you
won't soon forget it.**

A "character void" exists in American culture today. There has been a "massaging down" of what is right and wrong. Situational ethics abound and the idea that there are certain basic "absolutes" to live by has become cliché and considered intolerant. Everyday the news reports on irregularities in government, corruption in business and scandals in the church.

I believe that these are symptoms of a major character "meltdown" in America. A "meltdown" that left unchecked, will ultimately eliminate our trust in these institutions and in our fellow man. When we can no longer trust one another, the very fabric of our society will be destroyed.

No modern man in America has exemplified "character" more than Dallas Cowboys and Pro Football Hall of Fame Coach, Tom Landry. He once said, *"A team with character needs no motivation."* As a man of character, he was motivated to do right things with his life, whatever the arena he happened to be in. Much has been documented about his accomplishments as a man, husband, father and coach. Having had the good fortune of working closely with Tom Landry for over ten years, I witnessed his character in action in some very unique ways during some very difficult times. I was never disappointed and always inspired.

I first met Tom Landry in November 1987; I was thirty-one years of age. It was the final stages of my interview process for the position of Director of the Greater Dallas Fellowship of Christian Athletes. Coach Landry was the Chairman of the Greater Dallas FCA board and we met at his office at the Dallas Cowboys facility in Valley Ranch. Oh, I had seen Coach Landry before in the community, but this was entirely different. As "corny" as it may sound, this was my personal hero and as a former football coach, my professional role model. Needless to say, I was just a little nervous.

The first thing I noticed upon meeting Coach Landry was just how physically big a man he was. Dressed in very stylish business attire (shirt, tie, etc.), he looked in fabulous physical condition, tall, firm jaw line and very strong. Over the years, you would not believe the number of people who, after meeting Coach Landry for the first time, would tell me, "I never knew he was such a big man." I guess standing on the sidelines with all of those big football players in complete uniform gave people the impression he was average size. Long, tall, Texan surely fit this man from Mission, Texas.

I was so nervous, that I really can't even remember the details of the conversation. What I do remember is that he was one of the most gracious human beings I had ever met, personable and the perfect gentleman. Well, I got the job and as time passed, Coach Landry and I became comfortable with each other. I am still amazed to think that, other than his assistant coaches, no one worked closer with him than I did for the next ten years. That ten-year journey forever impacted my life as I saw so many of the attributes of my Savior, lived out by a real man, a man's man, a gentle man, a man of character who just happened to be my personal hero.

The Landry influence goes far, wide and deep throughout the lives of the many people he knew and worked with him. Not to even mention the scores of people all over America who so admired how he lived his life that they sought to model their coaching philosophy, management principles or personal disciplines after this man from "Mission" whose life journey became a "mission" for his Heavenly Father. This was the one true goal that meant the most to the "Man in the Hat" and which he pursued with faith, determination, dignity and above all else, "Character."

"The world doesn't stop when you lose. You must think about the good things that happened to you. You must look ahead.

- Tom Landry

Chapter 1
Character Requires Faith in God

As a football player and coach, Tom Landry experienced a great deal of success very early in life. A football scholarship to the University of Texas where he not only met the love of his life Alicia, but also played on teams that had both Sugar Bowl and Orange Bowl victories. He was All-Pro as a professional and won an NFL Championship before the age of thirty-three. However, Coach Landry said, "*after the excitement wore off of each success, I still had an empty feeling in my life. That emptiness was made full in 1959 when I entered into a personal relationship with Jesus Christ.*"

I remember hearing Dallas Cowboys legend and Hall of Famer, Bob Lilly telling the story about the first team meeting at his first training camp in 1961. Lilly said he was anxiously waiting to be inspired by his new head coach when Coach Landry announced to the team that they needed to understand what his priorities in life were. They were "*God, family, and football.*" Lilly said he thought to himself, *"We'll never win a game!"* Bob Lilly, who was awarded the title of "Mr. Cow-

boy" by the fans, went on to fully understand the character
that set Coach Landry apart from so many had its foundation
in understanding the true priorities in life.

Apart from family, the Fellowship of Christian Athletes
was Tom Landry's number one ministry priority. FCA gave
him the platform to share his faith and he believed fervently
in reaching the youth of America with the Gospel message of
Jesus Christ. Coach Landry felt that most of a person's character was developed in their youth and therefore having them
trust Christ early in life was of vital importance. He once said
that "*Character was the most important determinant of a person's
success, achievement and ability to handle adversity.*" Additionally, Coach Landry was quoted as saying, "*Give me a choice
between an outstanding athlete with poor character and a lesser
athlete with good character, and I'll choose the latter every time.
The athlete with good character will often perform to his fullest
potential and be a successful football player while the outstanding
athlete with poor character will usually fail to play up to his potential and often won't achieve average performance.*"

These are the words of a man who knew something
about character, having crash-landed a B-17 during World
War II. The crash landing happened over Belgium, when after
a bombing run, the plane ran out of gas and he had to set it
down in a wooded area, which literally stripped the wings off
the fuselage. You see, true character requires faith in God.
One of Coach Landry's favorite Bible passages came from the
book of Romans, Chapter 5, verses 3-4 which says "*Not only
so, but we rejoice in our sufferings, because we know that suffering
produces perseverance; perseverance, character; and character hope.
–NIV.*" With a right relationship with our Heavenly Father,
our adversities in life should follow that sequence; "sufferings"

(adversities) produce "perseverance." Perseverance grows our "character" (who we really are) and with character we will have "hope" to deal with the issues of our lives.

As the senior staff person for Greater Dallas FCA, I worked closely with Coach Landry in his role as Board Chairman. Because of Landry's leadership, the Dallas FCA program had grown to be the largest single FCA program in America with an outreach to literally thousands of young athletes and coaches in schools throughout the Dallas area each week and through a comprehensive summer sports camping program throughout America. That growth required us to work long and hard at raising the funds to keep FCA staff and programs functioning.

A major component of the annual FCA fundraising effort was the Tom Landry FCA Open golf tournament. Under the leadership of Jim Myers (longtime Assistant Head Coach of the Dallas Cowboys under Landry) the tournament had grown to be the largest charity tournament not associated with a professional golf tour event in Texas. Other than Tom Landry, no individual did more to advance the FCA in Dallas than Jim Myers.

He remains a true unsung hero and Coach Landry loved and respected him very much as Jim exemplified the very essence of character and commitment. On a personal level, I am forever indebted to him for his tireless work to help reach the youth of our community for Christ.

Early in my FCA career, we were seeking a major sponsorship for the tournament from a large banking institution, which is now one of the largest banks in America. Coach Landry and I had scheduled an appointment to meet with the person in charge of such sponsorships. I arrived to the appointment just a few minutes before the scheduled time and discovered that Coach Landry was running a little late. Upon walking into the bank executive's office, it was obvious that he was originally from India or Pakistan.

I became a little nervous about the meeting, because so many public companies would decline financial support of FCA because of the Christian mission and we needed the money. My mind began to draw conclusions about how this meeting would end. I thought, "There is no way we are going to get a financial sponsorship from this guy." After all he is from India or Pakistan, probably Hindu or Muslim and not going to help out a Christian ministry like FCA. While waiting for Coach Landry he asked about FCA and I began an eloquent discourse of all the redeeming values of FCA as an organization. FCA built character, provided "positive peer pressure" and gave kids a place to learn about being good citizens, so on and so forth, all the time wishing, praying that Coach Landry would soon arrive.

After what seemed to me to be an eternity, even though it was only about ten or fifteen minutes, Coach Landry arrived. After the introductions and just a few minutes of the standard small talk, Coach sat up in his chair, leaned over the bank executive's desk and proclaimed to the bank executive, *"You have to share Christ with these kids; it's the only hope for America. We hope you'll help us."* You can't imagine the spirit of conviction that came over me at that moment. We left shortly thereafter and guess what, we received a check for $25,000 within just a week or so for the sponsorship that we needed.

I was humbled in a mighty way that day and learned a lesson from the Coach that I have never forgotten. You see, I had proclaimed all the secular and humanistic virtues of FCA and my fear of rejection and not receiving the money prevented me from proclaiming what really mattered, that, *"God so loved the world that He gave his only begotten Son, that whoever believes in Him should not perish, but have eternal life"* (John 3:16).

You have seen the verse many times at all sorts of sporting venues in our country. Its simple truth is of everlasting value. Make no mistake, Tom Landry was a bold witness for his Savior, because he knew that hope for America and all mankind lies in the person of Jesus Christ. I never saw him reject the opportunity to proclaim the truth about the Gospel message. From that day forward I never apologized or "beat around the bush" when it came to telling anyone who we approached to know that we needed their financial help to reach the great mission field that existed with the youth of America, for Jesus Christ. That day my faith was misplaced, Tom Landry's faith however, was firmly planted in the hands of his Heavenly Father.

Character Requires Faith in God
– Ken Horton

When the leaders of the early church wanted believers to grasp the significance of faith in Jesus, they consistently anchored the discussion with a man named Abraham.[1] Responding to God's clear direction, Abram (meaning *exalted father*) left his home in Ur,[2] traveled north along the Euphrates River, buried his father in Haran,[3] and then followed God's leadership as a 75-year-old to a place he had never been before. In that land, known as Canaan, God promised to make him into a great nation and through him to bless all the nations of the world. Though he certainly stumbled along the way,[4] his confidence in God continued to grow. God changed his name to Abraham (meaning *father of many nations*) and he became a model of faith for the rest of human history. His faith in God's promise of a son with his wife, Sarah, was realized in the birth of Isaac when he was one hundred years old. About fifteen to twenty years later, his faith was supremely tested when he was told to sacrifice his beloved Isaac. This drama in Genesis 22 provides the proto-type for God's ultimate provision for our sin through the sacrifice of Jesus Christ, God's Son, on that same mountain two thousand years later.

What do we learn from Abraham's life? First, he had the *faith to start* to obey God's direction even when the destina-tion was not clear. The path of faith begins with the first step of believing that we can experience forgiveness and eternal life through faith in Jesus Christ's death for us. Second, he had the *faith to follow*. Like all of us, Abraham stumbled. But he continued to take the next step with God who was faithful to strengthen him as his faith matured. Finally, he had *faith to finish*. In Hebrews 11:6 we learn that *"without faith it is impos-sible to please God."* It is not the amount of faith that deter-mines our destiny... it is the object of our faith. When we trust God and His provision through Jesus, we join Abraham, Tom Landry and millions more who have discovered that trusting God never leads to disappointment.

Personal Training

1. What does having faith mean to you?

2. In what people or things have you placed your faith? Make a list of these.

_____, _____,

_____, _____.

3. How have you been disappointed in the people or things you have had faith in?

4. Read Hebrews 11:1. How is faith described in this passage of scripture? Now read the entire chapter.

5. What insights or new perspectives about faith come to mind?

"The only way a person can really become strong is to have setbacks."

- Tom Landry

Chapter 2

Character in the Face of Insurmountable Odds

As I stated at the beginning of this book, *"Character is a difficult thing to describe, but once you have seen it, you won't soon forget it."* Think about an act of character you witnessed or learned from history that has made an impression on you for a moment. Personally, I am reminded of a story I once heard from the sports arena about New York Yankees Manager Joe McCarthy. From 1932 to 1942 under McCarthy's leadership the Yankees were in eight World Series and won seven. That's a pretty phenomenal run of championships. As much as a Texas boy hates to admit it, the Yankees probably are the true "America's Team" even though I am a holdout for the Dallas Cowboys under Tom Landry.

A newspaper reporter that traveled with the Yankees had a pre-game discussion with McCarthy one day. He asked the Yankees Manager what made the team so good. McCarthy did not answer immediately, instead he called his shortstop over to the dugout where he and the reporter were sitting and asked, "What's your batting average?" The shortstop said, "I don't know." Next, he called over his top home run hitter and asked, "How many homers do you have?" The player answered, "Gee Skipper, I don't know." Finally, McCarthy called his best pitcher over and said, "What's your E.R.A.?" The pitcher looked puzzled at the question and answered, "I don't know, Skip." McCarthy then turned to the reporter and replied, *"Don't you get it now. They just come to beat you every-day."*

Well, being a former college baseball player, that story gets me "pumped!" In our culture where everything is "me, me, me," these responses are virtually unheard of. When is the last time you heard a news story about a professional athlete who put his own agenda aside for the betterment of the team? It takes a great sense of character to put team goals and others ahead of your own agenda.

Former Olympian, Dave Johnson has a story of great character. Dave Johnson was the best decathlete in the world as he prepared for the 1992 Olympic Games in Barcelona, Spain. During the Olympic trials, Dave began to experience some noticeable pain in his left foot. He qualified for the Olympics, but as the games rolled around, the nagging pain in his left foot was still there.

Dave Johnson was not only the best decathlete in the world at the time, he was a marketing icon for track and field. The 6-foot-4 Johnson was as handsome and "All American" as they come and his endorsement value was huge for American companies.

The pain in Johnson's foot during the first day of Olympic competition was excruciating. The premiere decathlete in the world and the guy favored to win "the Gold" was well in back of the leaders in points after that first day. Dave was so disappointed and the pain was so bad that he wanted to quit. Johnson's coach and others began to encourage him to finish the competition and give it his best. Finally through prayer and counsel from friends, Johnson decided to continue the next day. He put on a shoe that was two sizes larger, laced it up tight and during the next day's events came from well back in the field to win the bronze medal. It was later determined that Dave Johnson had actually won the bronze medal while competing with a stress fracture in his left foot. I can't even imagine the pain that Dave Johnson must have experienced. However, it was Johnson's inner character that allowed him to continue in spite of extreme physical pain. That bronze medal was really the gold medal when it came to character.

There are also great acts of character from World War II history. In the fall of 1940, the Battle of Britain was in full force and Germany bombed England and the London area for over 30 consecutive nights. Each and every day the English people literally "dug out" to keep up the fight. I simply can't comprehend how horrific an experience that was for those people. That took unbelievable character.

According to many World War II veterans the movie, "Saving Private Ryan," was the most accurate movie depiction of what it was really like at Normandy on D-Day. Seeing that movie humbled me and gave me a great appreciation for what the men and women of "The Greatest Generation" did for you and me. Can you imagine what must have been going through the minds of those young soldiers as they approached Omaha Beach in their landing crafts? All had to be scared, the young kids in uniform, as well as their older officers and non-commissioned officers. They were without question "sitting ducks." The character it took to advance in the face of that disadvantaged situation must have been enormous. Most of the veterans simply said they were just doing their job.

I have previously mentioned Tom Landry's quote, *"A team with character needs no motivation."*

American Statesman, Henry Clay once said, *"Of all the properties which belong to honorable men, not one is so highly prized as that of character."*

The great evangelist, D.L. Moody once said, *"Character is who you are in the dark."*

Tommy Nelson, pastor of Denton Bible Church takes it a step further and said, *"Character is who you are in private. Because who you are in private is who you are."*

Character is defined in Webster's dictionary as follows:

a. The complex of mental and ethical traits making
   a person or group
b. Reputation
c. Moral excellence and firmness

The truth is, God's desire for our lives involves inner qualities that ultimately affect our outward behavior.

The final days of Jesus' earthly life is well recorded in the four Gospels. On Thursday evening, Jesus ate the Passover dinner with His disciples where they argued about which one of them would be the most important. In order to make a crucial point, Jesus rose and washed their feet to demonstrate that they should serve one another. After the meal, Jesus instituted the symbolic meal that is known as the Lord's Supper, a rite to be observed until He would come again. Also, during this evening together, it was made clear that Judas would be Jesus' betrayer and he left to make the final arrangements to betray Christ. (source: Bible Almanac)

Later, Jesus and the remaining disciples left the upper room where they had been and came to the place where I believe that the greatest act of character that ever occurred happened without a large human audience or much "fanfare." It was in a place called Gethsemane. "Gethsemane," from the Greek word pronounced *geth-say-man-ay*, meaning *oil press*, was the name given to an olive orchard at the foot of the Mount of Olives. Many believe it to have been one of the favorite places that Jesus visited, and for me, was the scene of what I believe to be the greatest single act of character ever demonstrated. Ironically, the garden that literally meant "*oil press*" would be the scene of unspeakable pressure, the likes no person had ever known.

The Scriptures record that at Gethsemane, Jesus became sorrowful and deeply distressed. Jesus then said to His disciples, "*My soul is exceedingly sorrowful, even to death.*" The very depth of the Savior's soul is troubled beyond anything we can even comprehend. Jesus then walked a little farther and fell to the ground on His face and prayed, "*O My Father, if it is possible, let this cup pass from me, nevertheless, not as I will, but as You will.*"

Obviously, under severe emotional pressure, when He found the disciples sleeping, He could not believe it and rebuked them for not staying awake. Real pressure has a way of making us lash out, because real pressure makes us feel isolated and we want others to understand our pain.

Jesus went away a second time and prayed, "*Oh My Father, if this cup cannot pass away from Me unless I drink it, Your will be done."* Returning again to where the disciples were, He found them asleep again. I get a picture of someone pacing back and forth searching for answers, searching for relief. He left where they were again, and prayed the same thing for a third time. After that, Jesus returned to the disciples and woke them because the time of his betrayal and arrest was at hand.

I can relate to disappointment and suffering. Several years ago, my marriage fell apart which led to divorce and joint custody of my two beautiful daughters Kelly and Jenna whom I love dearly with all my heart. I was in great personal despair and yes, "exceedingly sorrowful." How could the thing I wanted most in life, marriage and family, end in failure? Every kind of thought ran through my mind, even the thought of ending it all. People would tell me to just try to live, "one day at a time," but I was struggling to live hour to hour. I remember walking into stores and becoming disoriented, actually forgetting why I was there.

It was about 9 p.m. one evening and I was crying out to God like never before. I was begging Him to minister to me, to ease the pain, to bring encouragement and give me hope. Sitting down, I picked up my Bible and began skimming through it, all the while asking God to give me something from His Word that I could hold on to. Oh, I had heard of people doing similar things and God revealing treasure from His truth to meet the need at hand, but it had never happened to me and in fact, I was generally skeptical of those who had such stories.

While flipping through the Bible, Matthew, chapter 26 seemed to suddenly jump off the pages. More specifically, the account of Jesus in the Garden of Gethsemane that I have been discussing with you. I read these scriptures that I had read before, and heard more than one sermon on, with an understanding I never before had. What was going on here? How could Jesus be so distressed? After all, He was the Messiah, God's Son. The book of Colossians says that, *"For by Him all things were created that are in heaven and that are on earth, visible and invisible, whether thrones or dominions or principalities or powers. All things were created through Him and by Him"* (Colossians 1:19). Jesus is literally ruler over the *"cosmos"* and yet felt such distress that Luke wrote, His sweat was like drops of blood. Have you ever sweated blood over something?

The word "cup" kept jumping out to me as I read the Gethsemane account. Three times Jesus agonized over the "cup." Over the years I just assumed that the "cup" simply referred to the events that were about to happen to Him, arrest, betrayal, humiliation, scourging, beating and finally the most dreaded of all executions, crucifixion. That night in my despair, God revealed to me a truth I have never forgotten, a truth that gave me a depth of understanding about the Christian faith I had never before understood. It was all about the "cup." I glanced down at the notes in my Study Bible and there it was, an explanation of the "cup."

The term "cup" you see, is Hebrew symbolism meaning the full wrath of God against sin. It hit me like a ton of bricks. Who better to know the full wrath of God against sin than God Himself; Jesus? Fully God and yet fully man at the same time, a member of the triune God, ruler of the cosmos. I don't believe that Jesus was in agony over the arrest, betrayal, scourging and crucifixion. In fact, as He was being arrested, Peter cuts off the ear of the servant of the high priest who was part of the "multitude" there to arrest Jesus. Jesus rebukes

Peter for such an action reminding him that He could call down more than twelve legions of angels at anytime. The arrest and all that was humanly associated with the events to come was not the pain Jesus was most concerned about.

I believe Jesus completely understood that "the cross," "the cup," and "the full wrath of God against sin" was so severe that in his "flesh" and His knowledge of what was to come that He simply did not want to endure it, yet he willingly did.

Because of the character Jesus demonstrated in that place called Gethsemane, those who have placed their faith in Him for their eternal salvation will never experience the full wrath of God against sin. We cannot even begin to fathom what that wrath might be like. Jesus Christ took it all for you and me.

That night, "character" took on a whole new meaning for me as God ministered to me through His Word and the actions of my Savior. I realized four important truths about character that were demonstrated by Jesus in the Garden of Gethsemane:

1. Character is the ability to wait patiently and put your desires aside for the good of others.
2. Character is walking with God out of obedience, when your mind and spirit don't want to.
3. Character is the ability to suffer rejection and injustice but still walk uprightly before God, not because it is easy, but because it is right.
4. Character is the ability to humble yourself while others seem to be on top, knowing that God has a time and place to exhibit His power through you.

Suddenly, the pain I was going through seemed quite small in comparison to what my Savior went through. Not because He was forced to, but because He loved me and was obedient to the will of His Heavenly Father. I felt a hope, I felt a heart of thankfulness... and then I cried. *"Character is difficult to define, but once you have seen it, you won't soon forget it."*

I have gone back many, many times to that act of character demonstrated by Jesus since that night. Focusing on it, instead of my own circumstances, seems to shed a light on my life that gives me the strength to endure the difficult times because of the great love Jesus has for me.

Character in the Face of Insurmountable Odds
– Ken Horton

"...because My servant Caleb has a different spirit and follows me wholeheartedly, I will bring him into the land he went to, and his descendents will inherit it." (Numbers 14:24 NIV)

Where his contemporaries saw giant obstacles, Caleb saw great opportunity. When they pulled back in fear, he surged forward in bold faith. God's affirmation in the verse above stimulates our careful examination of Caleb's character. How can we be "different" and "follow God wholeheartedly"?

Character qualities for such a life leap from the biblical

account of Caleb's leadership among the Israelites. First, he was a man of *credibility* and *availability*. When leaders were needed[5] to explore Canaan, Caleb was the person selected from Judah's tribe. He had already gained the confidence of his contemporaries and did not flinch when he was chosen for this dangerous mission. Setting the pace during the everyday challenges of life positioned Caleb to face the giant adversaries in Canaan.

Second, Caleb was *honest* about the difficulties that would be met as they entered the Promised Land. He did not minimize the perils, affirming with all the spies the presence of fortified cities and powerful opponents. Naïve optimism that discounts the challenges we face is an expression of folly, not faith. Caleb saw the giants clearly, but he believed that God's direction to enter the land included His power to overcome the giants.[6]

Caleb's honesty was balanced by his *boldness*. When Caleb and Joshua stood against the faithless and fearful majority report ("we seemed like grasshoppers in our own eyes"),[7] Caleb and Joshua declared their fearless confidence in God.[8] When facing insurmountable odds, the courage to take a stand against the crowd is essential. The bottom line for Caleb's boldness was, "The Lord is with us."

Fear and folly have sobering consequences. For almost forty years Caleb and Joshua watched as all their fellow spies (and millions of others) died in the wilderness.[9] After this decades-long death march in the wilderness, Joshua and Caleb shared the delight of entering Canaan with a new generation of Israelites.[10] As an 85 year-old, Caleb could have basked in the glow of his honored role of leadership a generation earlier. But when given a choice, he claimed the area in

Canaan where the giants lived.[11] He had remained physically and spiritually vigorous for forty years, so he could fulfill God's purpose in his life. This combination of *passion* and *endurance* enabled Caleb to experience God's greatest blessings in his last years.

Ready to face insurmountable odds? Learn from Caleb as you wholeheartedly follow the Lord.

Personal Training

1. What does having faith mean to you?

2. What are your thoughts on the following statement:

"Character is difficult to describe, but once you have seen it you won't soon forget it."

3. Who is a person of "character" that you know and admire? List a few of their character qualities.

_____, _____,

_____, _____.

4. How is character revealed in the lives of people?

5. How are "faith" and "character" intertwined?

6. Read Romans 5:1-5. What does this say to you about character?

7. What is a personal character quality you need to work on?

"A team with character needs no motivation."

- Tom Landry

Chapter 3
Character Requires True Humility

After 29 years, the only coach in Dallas Cowboys history was released in 1989. I had actually been in Coach Landry's office on FCA business the same week the story would break and he did not give any indication that a potential storm was brewing. I am confident that he had to have some indication that a change could possibly take place. However, that too, is another great character trait of the "Man in the Hat." He was cool under pressure. I guess flying B-17's in World War II can do that for you.

Tom Landry's humility was simply amazing. Being one of the most recognizable and popular people in all of sports, did not seem to affect Coach Landry, as I never saw him take on the "celebrity" persona. He was a man of pretty humble beginnings and was just a solid servant of God. If Coach Landry had been a small town rancher or businessman, he simply would have strived to be the best rancher or business-man he could be, no frills, just solid work ethic and Christian values.

I remember a story told by football coach David Knaus.

David was an outstanding football player at San Antonio Churchill High School in the early 1970's and then Texas Tech University. David and I got to know each other when he joined the SMU football staff under head coach, Tom Rossley, in the early 1990's. David attended an FCA summer camp while in high school. Coach Landry happened to be a part of that camp as a featured speaker. David said the biggest impression on him from that camp was the fact that during free time one day, he went to the swimming pool, jumped in and looked around and guess what, there was Coach Landry in the pool with the rest of the teenagers and adult volunteers.

He was so impressed that this NFL Head Football coach was willing to fully participate and interact with the campers on such a basic level that he never forgot it. The "Man in the Hat" was a Super Bowl winning coach, but truly humble.

We decided to do a major fundraising event for Greater Dallas FCA one year to honor Coach Landry's 70th birthday. When we approached him about the idea, with utmost sincerity, Coach Landry said, "Do you think anyone would come?" Well, we did the event on the floor of Texas Stadium. The event included entertainer Louise Mandrell, William Bennett (U.S. Secretary of Education), many former players and hundreds of friends and fans. The event raised $400,000 for Greater Dallas FCA. Coach Landry was "blown away" by the event, because he originally did not think anyone would be interested.

There was another time shortly after Coach Landry left the Dallas Cowboys that I thought demonstrated how humble he really was. It was at a FCA Tom Landry Associates Weekend in Phoenix, Arizona. Tom Landry Associates were major donors from all over America who had made major financial gifts to FCA. Every Fall, this group of people would be invited to a special weekend somewhere in America where the Dallas Cowboys would be playing. The weekend was designed for FCA fellowship and building into the lives of these donors as "teammates" in the work of FCA. It would consist of great platform speakers, playing golf and attending a Dallas Cowboys game. The Cowboys game was always a part of the weekend, because for years the weekend took place when Coach Landry was walking those sidelines for the team in Silver and Blue. The Coach would literally take the time out of his schedule during football season to be a part of this event at the city where they were playing.

This happened to be the year after Coach Landry had been dismissed from the Cowboys. The event had already been booked and yes there was a Dallas Cowboys game as a part of the weekend activities. I attended the Tom Landry Associates Weekend that year in my role as the Greater Dallas FCA Director. It was a great time that included golf at Karsten Solhiem's (FCA National Trustee and founder of PING Golf) golf course and an evening event on Saturday night that included Arizona Cardinals Head Coach, Gene Stallings and entertainer Glen Campbell.

As Sunday rolled around, I began to wonder if Coach Landry would attend the game with these FCA donors. The donors of course were "fired up" to be going to the Cowboys – Cardinals game, but it probably was not something Coach Landry would want to do. Also, his celebrity status was so strong, if he attended, I thought he would probably be sitting in a box somewhere in Sun Devils Stadium, where the Cardinals played back then.

We had breakfast at the hotel and then the charter buses

rolled up to transport everyone to Tempe for the game. While I sat down in my seat on the bus, Coach Landry steps on the bus, dressed in casual attire just like everyone else and off we went to the game. I thought that when we got there, Coach would probably be whisked off to a box or at least very special seating. The buses pulled up to the stadium and we all exited and started walking to the gate. Coach Landry was right with us and much to my surprise, walked right in that stadium just like every other person that day and he made his way with us to our group's seats, which were really not all that good from a location standpoint. Coach did wear a golf cap and sunglasses, but yes there was a lot of head turning and pointing that day. We sat the whole afternoon, watching that Dallas Cowboys – Arizona Cardinals game. Coach Landry was there the whole time with our group, interacting with everybody just like he was "one of the guys" on a Sunday outing. I thought to myself, "I wonder when the last time this man, the third winningest coach in the entire history of the National Football League and soon to be member of the Pro Football Hall of Fame, sat like a typical fan in the 'cheap seats' at a professional football game?" He did it because of his strong belief in FCA. His humility was simply beyond compare.

You will recall that I mentioned the great success of the Tom Landry FCA Open Golf Tournament. Many years of hard work had been put into making the tournament the premier charity tournament in Texas. It was usually held the third or fourth Monday in April. It was so prominent in the community that most charity tournaments waited for our announcement date before scheduling their tournaments. Dallas is a big golf town come Spring and everyone is getting in the mood for the Byron Nelson Golf Classic and wanting to play golf. That's one of the reasons we held the tournament during that time of year, along with the fact that it fit Coach Landry's schedule well. The tournament had become a mainstay in the community. Tom Landry FCA Open charity tournament in April, then the Byron Nelson Golf Classic each Spring.

Wouldn't you know it, "Murphy's Law," the newly created, Jimmy Johnson Foundation (named for the new Dallas Cowboys Coach) announces to the public the date of their inaugural golf tournament and it is on the same day as the Tom Landry FCA Open golf tournament. We let the Jimmy Johnson Foundation know of the conflict and after deliberation, it was decided that we would move the date of the Tom Landry FCA Open back to be played one week after the Jimmy Johnson tournament. After we advised the folks at the Jimmy Johnson Foundation of our decision, they were kind enough to invite us to their pre-tournament party and auction the night before the tournament. Additionally, they suggested that two footballs each having signatures of Tom Landry, Roger Staubach, Jimmy Johnson and Troy Aikman be auctioned off during the live auction portion of the evening with the proceeds going to the Fellowship of Christian Athletes as a "thank you" for moving the Landry tournament date. This was a very kind gesture and we all agreed.

The Jimmy Johnson Foundation pre-tournament party was held at a hotel in Grapevine, Texas on a Sunday night before the tournament. The golf tournament was a celebrity format and the Jimmy Johnson Foundation had secured quite a few former NFL stars to participate in the tournament. They gave FCA a very nice table that was filled with me,

Coach Landry, Jim Myers and some other key FCA volunteers. To this day, I will never forget how Coach Landry's presence there made a huge impact for Christ. I also remember a somewhat humorous moment when many of Jimmy Johnson's assistant coaches came up to our table to meet Coach Landry. They were like little kids.

Dallas Cowboys Assistant Coach, Dave Campo in particular was quite cute. I always thought Campo, who would later become Head Coach of the Cowboys, was a really good guy. Not a very tall man, maybe 5-foot-7, Campo stepped up to our table where Coach Landry was sitting and bent down a little and said, "Mr. Landry, my name is Dave Campo and I coach the defensive secondary for the Dallas Cowboys. I just wanted to meet you and tell you how much I have admired you." The respect he had for Tom Landry was obviously pretty significant. He said, "Mr. Landry," not "Coach Landry" or "Tom." As usual, the Coach was totally gracious, but I had to believe he was a little amused as well, because Campo seemed like a kid asking for an autograph instead of an NFL coach introducing himself. Such was the great presence of the "Man in the Hat."

The program started and was hosted by Roy Firestone who was at the time a very popular sports show host on ESPN. A remarkable set of events began to unfold. Firestone, an extremely talented entertainer/comedian in his own right, suddenly announced that he was so glad to be there that night to help raise money for the Fellowship of Christian Athletes. Whoa! I thought. That was a major slip of the tongue. This was the Jimmy Johnson Golf Tournament to raise money for the Jimmy Johnson Foundation. A few minutes later he said it again. I thought surely somebody is going to tell him of the error and it wouldn't happen again.

Well, as part of the evening, a few former NFL stars turned sportscasters were on the program to say a few words and thank people for participating in the tournament. Joe Thiesman, former Washington Redskins quarterback gets up and takes the microphone from Roy Firestone and proceeds to tell the crowd that he couldn't think of a better thing to do than raise money for the Fellowship of Christian Athletes. I thought to myself, this is unbelievable! A few minutes later, Pat Summerall, former NFL star and at the time lead football broadcaster for CBS and later FOX, gets up and said the same thing. All of a sudden this evening had become all about he Fellowship of Christian Athletes.

Shortly thereafter the live auction started and it came time to bid on the two footballs signed by Landry, Staubach, Johnson and Aikman. As an added incentive to get the bidding going, the four of them went up on stage holding the footballs. Make no mistake; these footballs were unique collector items and whoever bought the footballs would also get their picture taken with the four sports figures. The bidding was "hot" to say the least and Roy Firestone was really making a big deal about the footballs, the Fellowship of Christian Athletes and the four men standing on the stage who had signed the footballs.

I focused on Coach Landry the whole time. I could tell he was uncomfortable being up there, but I doubt if anyone else picked up on it. Then I thought to myself; that this was probably the last place he wanted to be, up on stage at someone else's fundraiser, raising funds for his number one charitable endeavor, the Fellowship of Christian Athletes. However in the final analysis, Coach Landry did it for FCA. He did it for

FCA because to him, FCA meant reaching America's youth with the Gospel of Jesus Christ and he loved his Savior.

The bidding wrapped up and $25,000 was raised for FCA with those two footballs. More importantly, because of the great humility of Tom Landry, the Fellowship of Christian Athletes and ultimately Christ was lifted up at the Jimmy Johnson Golf Tournament party. I believe wholeheartedly that God intervened that night amongst all the party hoopla to honor the humility of a true celebrity who was simply the most humble man I have ever known… "The Man in the Hat."

Character Requires True Humility
– Ken Horton

"Now Moses was a very humble man, more humble than anyone else on the face of the earth." Numbers 12:3 NIV

How do you become "more humble than anyone else on the face of the earth"? Moses' life provides stimulating insight into this provocative question. Moses was *trained to lead* as an adopted son of Pharaoh's daughter. He had the wisdom of Egypt at his disposal, "powerful in speech and action." [12] His first attempt to give leadership to the Israelites was a catastrophe. Relying only on his strength he avenged the mistreatment of his people by killing an Egyptian.[13] When he then sought to bring reconciliation to two Israelites the next day, they rejected his help and exposed his crime.[14]

Fleeing like a common criminal, this prince of Egypt had learned the first lesson of humility: *Strength alone has destruc-*

tive consequences. He endured forty years in the desert of Midian, shepherding sheep and raising a family. As an eighty year old Moses had lost his ambition to lead, but not his capabilities to do so. God appeared to Moses as a burning bush with a clear message, "Go...bring the Israelites out of Egypt."[15] Drawn into the leadership role, squirming all the way,[16] Moses displayed a severe sense of inadequacy. Humility is not a lack of confidence, but clarity about our source of confidence. In the midst of his objections Moses finally grasped this essential for humility and journeyed back to Egypt.

During the drama of ten plagues, which fell on Egypt as Pharaoh refused to release the Israelites,[17] Moses faced the most powerful man on earth and prevailed through God's strength. When the Israelites stood before the Red Sea, Moses declared, "Do not be afraid. Stand firm and you will see the deliverance the Lord will bring you today."[18] Moses discovered that humility is the doorway to prevailing strength which honors God while accomplishing His purposes.

During their journey toward the Promised Land, Moses' humility was tested in a unique way. While God was giving Moses the Law on Mount Sinai the Israelites became impatient and convinced Aaron to build a golden calf for them to worship.[19] God tested Moses by suggesting that all the Israelites be wiped out because of this grievous sin. He offered Moses the opportunity to become the beginning of a new nation.[20] Moses passed this test because he valued God's reputation as a faithful God more than his own renown as a spiritual leader.[21] Humility shines brightest when honoring God is our highest value. Did Moses make mistakes? Certainly, one even cost him the opportunity to enter the Promised Land.[22] But he left a pattern for humility that will guide us toward a life that honors God.

Personal Training

1. How have you defined "humility" throughout your life? What is the opposite of "humility"?

2. What does "false humility" look like?

3. Have you ever admired the "humility" of another person? Why?

4. Read James: 4:1-10. James quotes Proverbs 3-34 in this passage of scripture. What attitude should we have in our relationship to God? Why is this important?

5. Read John 13:1-19. What do these verses say to you about humility? What are some other ways Jesus Christ demonstrated "humility" during his life on earth?

*"Leadership is getting someone to do what they don't want to do,
to achieve what they want to achieve."*

- Tom Landry

Chapter 4

Character Requires the
Courage to Acknowledge Your Humanity

I often reminisce about my days of working with Coach Landry in FCA. Sometimes I reminisce and laugh a little at some of the fun times we had together, the witty things that Coach would say that surprised me and the funny situations that happened involving the so called "stoic," "stone faced," "Man in the Hat."

In December of 1988, UCLA came to town to play in the Annual Cotton Bowl Classic versus Texas A&M. UCLA just happened to have a big strong kid at quarterback named Troy Aikman. The Fellowship of Christian Athletes conducted an annual breakfast during the week of the Cotton Bowl game that actually had grown to be the largest event during the week, other than the game itself. I would sometimes attend the team practices along with my FCA staff to encourage the coaches and players and to meet the athletes scheduled to be on our breakfast program.

This year, UCLA was conducting their practices at Texas Stadium. It was quite cold that day in Dallas and as I arrived on the sideline to watch practice and interact with the team, "lo and behold" there was Coach Landry standing on the sideline in a full-length winter coat and customary "fedora hat." You have seen this image many times if you grew up watching the Dallas Cowboys play football. Alongside Coach was Gil Brandt, the Cowboys Director of Player Personnel. Brandt had really made a name for himself as a scout who found great football talent in the most peculiar of places. Recent Pro-Football Hall of Fame inductee, Rayfield Wright is just one example. Has there ever been another NFL player out of Fort Valley State University in Georgia? Or, what about Jethro Pugh coming out of Elizabeth City State University in North Carolina? Brandt knew how to find the talent and Coach Landry would "pull the trigger" on whether or not to draft the player.

I walked up to Coach Landry and Gil said hello, talked a minute and then the three of us stood there watching the UCLA practice, making a few comments about players, etc. Coach Landry was obviously there to personally take a look at Troy Aikman and Gil Brandt was almost "giddy" as both knew that the Cowboys were positioned in the upcoming NFL draft to take Aikman as their number one pick. The Cowboys were coming off a 3-13 season and in need of another great quarterback to continue the legacy of great quarterbacks like Don Meredith, Roger Staubach and Danny White. Coach Landry was working hard to re-build the Cowboys after that 3-13 season. It should be noted however that the 3-13 team was much better than that record indicated. They were very competitive that year and lost 5-6 games in the fourth quarter, mainly due to inexperience at some key positions, like quarterback. That 3-13 team could have easily been 8-8 or 9-7, but the record book does not record anything but the wins and losses. Also, most people don't know that it was Coach Landry who had drafted future NFL stars Michael Irvin (now a member of the Pro Football Hall of Fame) and Ken Norton Jr. just a year earlier who, along with eleven other Landry players would be the nucleus for Jimmy Johnson's first Super Bowl Championship team.

Additionally, many have soon forgotten that Coach Landry posted an NFL record 20 consecutive winning seasons with the Cowboys. This is an amazing record when you consider that the whole "draft system" is designed to provide parity in the league and prevent the development of team "dynasties." The teams with the worst records get first shot at the best college talent each year through the NFL draft. Make no mistake, Tom Landry was re-building the Dallas Cowboys and that was his motivation to continue to coach.

UCLA coach, Terry Donahue, was an energetic and very outgoing guy. As the UCLA practice concluded that day, Donahue called his team together in the middle of Texas Stadium and asked Coach Landry to come over. The three of us (Coach, Gil and I) walked over to the team, which was now on one knee, circled up in the middle of the field. Coach Donahue began to tell the team just how fortunate they were to have Tom Landry at their practice and began to recite all of Coach Landry's accomplishments. Then at the most unexpected time and literally out of nowhere, Donahue asks Coach Landry to say something to the team. Talk about surprise! Do you remember being in school and your mind being somewhere else when the teacher called on you? Multiply that by about 100 and you will be in the neighborhood at just how surprised Coach Landry was. The look on Landry's face was utter shock, with a little embarrassment. I know his mind had to be elsewhere, because he was so taken back and this wasn't a high school team, this was the UCLA Bruins, a team of young men who were waiting for the "Living Legend" to impart some message that would inspire them. The terms stoic and stone-faced were blown out of the water that day. Like a kid caught with his hand in the cookie jar, Coach Landry was totally "busted" to use a modern day phrase. Somehow he regained his composure and encouraged the team in their upcoming game. I must admit, there was a moment there when I was just more than a little nervous for the Coach.

Later, and many times afterward over the years, I have "chuckled" to myself as I recalled that scene. Landry's public persona was "stoic," "stern," "controlled" so on and so forth, that day Coach Landry was just another human being caught in a somewhat embarrassing moment. I tell this story because the Tom Landry I knew never thought too highly of himself and was as human as they came. He was not afraid to acknowledge his humanity or even laugh at himself. For some reason, I liked my personal hero more after that day, because I felt like I could relate to him. Much is the same with our Savior, Jesus Christ. He willingly became fully man while remaining fully God, out of love for you and me. It was in this way that He could fully relate to us and us to Him.

The "Man in the Hat" was quite witty. Are you surprised? I was initially and many people were.

The 1989 Cotton Bowl Classic would feature the Arkansas Razorbacks (you might already begin to sense something funny) and the Tennessee Vols. Arkansas' school colors are red and white, while Tennessee's are orange and white. Coach Landry was our featured speaker that year at the FCA Cotton Bowl breakfast. The program included both head coaches, Arkansas' Ken Hatfield (one of my favorite all time coaches and people) and Johnny Majors from Tennessee.

I had the privilege of introducing Coach Landry that morning and tried to share some personal insights about him that few would know and it was a little emotional for me. After all he was my personal hero and I had grown to love him as a brother in Christ. It was only a few months earlier that Landry had been fired by an Arkansas alumnus. My goal was to shed light on the fabulous things that Coach Landry did for FCA that few would know about other than me. Well, I got a little choked up, but made it through the introduction. The "sold out" crowd of 1,200 people was so quiet you could almost hear the proverbial "pin drop."

Coach Landry immediately stepped up to the podium, to "bail me out" a little and then the thunder of applause began for the Coach and yes, just one of many, many standing ovations I witnessed over the years for the Coach followed. The crowd finally settled down, Coach Landry thanked me, looked out at the crowd and said "I'm struggling just who to root for in this game." He said "You know I'm a Longhorn," then he looked at Johnny Majors and said "you know Tennessee's colors are orange and white" then he looked at Ken Hatfield and said "Arkansas is red and white," finally with perfect comedic timing he looked at the crowd and said "Sorry Ken, after what's happened to me in recent months, red just isn't my favorite color." Everyone in the audience knew what the reference was about. The crowed roared with laughter and the "Man in the Hat" was in control of that crowd like he was with his game plan each and every Sunday for those 29 years as Head Coach of the Dallas Cowboys. Tom Landry, the man, was not afraid to be human. I grew to love that more and more about him.

In 1991, Lisa Landry Childress, Coach Landry's youngest child was diagnosed with liver cancer while at the same time being pregnant with her first child. Lisa was a beautiful young woman with a strong and sincere faith in the Lord. As a father of two daughters myself, I can tell you that there truly is something special about dads and their daughters. Lisa was the baby of the family and it was very clear to me that she was a very special blessing to Coach Landry.

The cancer diagnosis was an obvious blow to Landry and the entire family. On top of that Lisa was pregnant and any cancer treatments could possibly harm the baby. Rather than risk the life of her child, Lisa made the decision to postpone treatment until the baby was born and placed her faith and trust in God's will for her life and the life of the baby. This took great courage and faith for both her and her husband Gary Childress. Lisa eventually gave birth to a healthy young girl they named Christina. After giving birth, the doctor's notified Lisa that her only option was to have a liver transplant. Within ten days of giving birth to Christina, Lisa received a Liver transplant. Lisa remained cancer free for about the next three years but on a routine follow-up exam once again learned that the cancer had returned.

I'll never forget the evening that Coach Landry called me at home to ask me to have the FCA staff and volunteers in Dallas and across America to join in prayer for Lisa. The stoic man that roamed the sidelines for all of those years was quite human that night as he shared his prayer request with all his heart. The very public, yet extremely private Tom Landry was not afraid to acknowledge his humanity and the great need he had for his baby girl. He was a father who hurt for what was happening to his girl, anxious and yet believed mightily in the will of his Heavenly Father.

Lisa went home to be with the Lord in 1995. The celebration of Lisa's life took place at the Landry's home church, Highland Park Methodist. The memorial service was beautiful and packed with family, friends and loved ones. After the service, Coach Landry stood outside the church by himself as a long line of people greeted him to express their sympathy regarding his great loss. I stood at just about the end of the line, in order for others to have a brief moment with the Coach. Eventually the line diminished and as I stepped up to Coach Landry, I could see the pain in his eyes and for the one and only time in our ten plus years of working together, he immediately embraced me with a complete hug. This was what I refer to as a "God moment." I did not see Coach Landry hug anyone who came through that line, but as soon as I arrived, he embraced me in the most human way I ever saw him. It was an embrace that lasted for several seconds and completely out of character for this "rock" of a man. I was truly blessed that God gave him the freedom to be a real living human being to me in that moment of pain.

I am emotional just thinking about that embrace as I write these words. We spoke for a minute and I, like so many others, expressed my deepest sympathy regarding the loss of Lisa. The Coach then immediately said to me, "Well, I know you understand loss." You will recall that I told you that my wife had ended our marriage and Coach Landry was referring to the loss of the love of my life. In his day of deepest sorrow, Tom Landry was actually trying to comfort me and minister to me about my divorce. I have often wondered if that very fact, gave him the freedom to embrace me that day, knowing that I did have some depth of understanding of his pain. The Word of God does tell us to "bear one another's burdens." We never spoke of it again, but that day, Tom Landry seemed to be the most human and honorable man I had ever known. In reality, I learned over the next several years, he really was.

Character Requires the Courage to Acknowledge Your Humanity
– Ken Horton

Two strong men expressing their loyal friendship and genuine compassion with a bear-hug embrace. A powerful moment for Tom Landry and Donnie Snyder…and for two of the heroes of Israel, Jonathan and David.[23] Though Jonathan's life was cut short in the backwash of his father's folly,[24] his loyal friend honored both Saul and Jonathan after their deaths[25] with an emotional vulnerability that revealed the depth of David's character.

David was described as a man after God's own heart.[26] This does not suggest he was morally superior. In fact, he was an adulterer and murderer.[27] But in the midst of life's distresses, many being self-inflicted, David ran toward God, poured out his heart to Him and received the help and hope only God can provide.[28]

Two encounters with relatives of Saul, who had repeatedly attempted to kill David, reveal the impact of this transparent vulnerability before God. After he became king, David sought out Jonathan's son, Mephibosheth, and showered kindness on him, treating him as part of his family.[29] With severe injuries to his feet and his family disgraced by Saul's kingship, Mephibosheth was vulnerable and David lavishly blessed him.[30]

Years later, as David fled Jerusalem in agonizing humiliation during the revolt by his son, Absalom, he encountered another man from Saul's family named Shimei. He cursed David, pelted him with stones and deserved the death David's men suggested. Instead David restrained his men and placed his own destiny in God's hands.[31] Even after the revolt is quelled by Absalom's death, David refuses to execute Shimei,[32] showing him the mercy David had experienced from God.

Our vulnerability with people reflects our vulnerability before God. Our kindness toward people reveals our gratitude for God's grace for us. Becoming this kind of person is a journey that is neither short nor pleasant. But it is the path toward becoming a person after God's heart.

Personal Training

1. What does it mean to "acknowledge your own humanity"? Why do you think it takes courage to do so?

2. Do you know someone who is "transparent" about the real issues in their life? How does that transparency make you feel?

3. Read Numbers 11:1-15. How did Moses acknowledge his humanity? How was Moses transparent before God?

4. Read Numbers 11:16-18. How did God respond to Moses' transparency about his humanity? What does this say to you about getting "real" with God about the inner issues of your life that you struggle with?

Bob Lilly
Pro Football Hall of Fame
Dallas Cowboys 1961-1974

Chapter 5

Character Requires
Commitment and Perseverance

My first thoughts upon meeting my new coach, Tom Landry, were that he was extremely polite, a true gentleman and that he looked very young, younger than any of my other coaches. Coach Landry was only 36 years of age when he became Head Coach of the newly formed NFL franchise team named the Dallas Cowboys. I also was instantly impressed with how lovingly he treated his wife, Alicia. Little did I know that the journey I was about to embark upon with this man named Landry would be one that would forever impact my life.

The year was 1961 and I had just come off an All-American year my senior season at Texas Christian University (TCU). As the number one draft pick of the Dallas Cowboys, I was very eager to start my professional career. Upon reporting to my first meeting for all the rookies, Coach Landry explained from the outset that his priorities in life were "God, Family and then Football." I thought to myself, *"This is messed up and we will never win a game."* Like so many other coaches I had known, I literally expected the *"devil,"* so to speak, to come out in Coach Landry. I thought that it was just a matter of time, at some point he would blow up and cuss us out, make some crude joke or do something that would demonstrate that those priorities were just a *"sham."* In all the years that I played for him and knew him, he never did. Tom Landry honored his Heavenly Father and he lived what he believed, day in and day out, season after season, before us all.

Today, I can tell you that Coach Landry had it exactly right and I believe those correct priorities not only made him successful in life and football, but impacted his players for years to come, long after their football careers were over. There is no doubt that Coach Landry created a football legacy with the Dallas Cowboys, but I believe that his greatest contribution was the human legacy that he created by living out his faith in Christ in such a consistent manner that the lives of his former players continue to be impacted by his Christ-like example today. I truly believe that of all the players that played for Coach Landry, there were quite a few that could have easily ended up in prison, had it not been for the father figure and great example that Coach Landry was to them. Everybody on the team respected him and most loved him, because he was totally consistent, he respected them as men, he did not play favorites and he always emphasized team.

Coached Landry never criticized his players in the press and a starter never automatically lost his position due to having to miss games because of injury. The starter once well, would immediately return to his starting position. He had to be "beat out" of his position by performance, not injury. All of us "hated the film room," however. This is where Coach Landry would point out team and individual mistakes from the last game. He was always quick to point out the successes as well. Seeing your "blunders" on the screen every week was a humbling experience, but you really learned from it and it helped you become a better player. Better players meant a better team and Coach Landry was always interested in what was best for the team.

Coach Landry loved to talk football and was innovative but at the same time was not afraid to borrow things from other teams. He studied the football philosophies of other coaches and this helped immensely in our preparation for our opponents. Coach Landry believed fully in the team concept and literally preached "faith" in the team's system and in your teammates. He charted our team and individual goals to determine trends and what to work on in practice and convinced us that the system would work if we had "faith" in it and in one another. Many former Dallas Cowboys became successful in business because they implemented the coaching principles that they learned under Coach Landry into their business endeavors. It was in many ways like getting an "MBA in business," while learning life lessons that would stay with you forever. I have always used those principles I learned from Coach Landry in both my personal and professional life. What an education it was!

Just a couple of years ago, while at the Pro Football Hall of Fame Game and induction ceremony, Marv Levy (former head coach of the Buffalo Bills) asked me and my former teammate, Mel Renfro, what is was like playing for Coach Landry. Mel summed it by saying

*"Coach Landry would tell me that if I would just believe in the
system and what he was saying that I would be successful. He
would tell me, that if I would look for a particular key, take a five
yard drop, my man would be there,"* Mel said, *"Sure enough, that
was the case every time."*

Coach Landry's game preparation was impeccable. Former teammate and All-Pro middle linebacker, Lee Roy Jor-
dan once told me, *"If Coach Landry spent all of his time coaching
the defense, no one would ever score on us."* I guess that's how we
got the nickname *"Doomsday Defense"* by the press. Terms like
"Football Genius" have been associated with Coach Landry
because of all of the innovations he brought to the game.
Having played for him for fourteen years, I believe he really
was.

Tom Landry was a "winner" and a great competitor. He
had won at every level he had competed on from high school,
through college at the University of Texas and on to his professional career with the New York Giants winning the NFL
Championship in 1956. The years 1960 thru 1965 had to be
tough years for him as losing was the norm for our new franchise, but not the core being of Tom Landry. He believed that
adversity provided the opportunity to become stronger, but
as we all know, constant adversity can take its "toll" on anyone.

The year was 1965 and *Sports Illustrated* had picked the
Dallas Cowboys to win the Eastern Divison of the National
Football League. Could this really be the year that all of those
losses and hard work in prior years had prepared us for? All
of us were feeling good about the prospects that lay before us,
but we started the season off in a bad way by losing several
games early in the season. We rolled into Pittsburg to play the

Steelers, had a bad game and recorded another loss. Instead of "chewing the team out" after the game, Coach Landry came into the locker room, apologized to the team for the bad start and personally accepted the responsibility for the bad start as our Head Coach. He then told us that he loved us, said he didn't know if he would be back next year and then broke down crying. Every man in that room was deeply touched that day, as we knew our Coach loved us and was not going to shirk his responsibility or blame his players for being unsuccessful on the field. Somehow, we knew his actions were not the "norm" in professional football and we rallied around our Coach, because deep down, we all knew we loved him too. We finished that 1965 season 7-7, which was quite a feat based on the start we had. In my opinion, that locker room experience was the true turning point for the Dallas Cowboys and Coach Landry's career, which would see him go on to be the third winningest coach in the entire history of the NFL.

Tom Landry was a man of great perseverance. We came back from that 1965 season to win the Eastern Division and play the Green Bay Packers in the 1966 title game in Dallas. The hard work and example set by Coach Landry was paying off. However, that game was the first of several "heartbreakers" for us as a team. It was a very close game that we had the chance to win in the last few seconds with the ball inside the Packers own five-yard-line. A penalty pushed us back and we were unable to get in the end zone and the Packers won. That season we finally proved to ourselves that we could be winners in the NFL.

The next season found us once again in the NFL Championship game against Packers in Green Bay, Wisconsin. We were going into the game feeling very prepared and really good. On top of that, the Packers were a little "beat up" with some injuries. It was 18 degrees on Saturday when we did our walk through and the field was in pretty good condition. George Andrie was my roommate that night and had gotten up early the next morning on game day at about 6:30 AM to attend mass. When he got back into the room, he took a glass of water and threw it on the window. It froze before it could get half way down the window. George said *"Bob, we are going to have to be leaders out there today."* It was about 13 degrees below zero with 35 mph winds making the wind chill somewhere in 30-40 degrees below zero range. George actually talked me into going out on the field for pre-game without a warm-up jacket to show our teammates that it wasn't that bad. When we walked out the door, I thought "you're crazy" and when we got back in, I put on long handled underwear and wrapped my feet and hands. The field was like an ice rink and as most remember we lost when Packers quarterback, Bart Starr ran a quarterback sneak in from the one yard line with 16 seconds left on the clock. Final score Green Bay 21 Dallas 17. Coach Landry came in the locker room and congratulated us for playing a great game under such adverse conditions. He was as "low" as I ever saw him. The plane ride back was a somber one and I remember looking out the window of the plane and just being thankful I was still alive and that we did not freeze to death. The "Ice Bowl" game set us back a couple of years, but Coach Landry's commitment and perseverance continued to pay off as we were in the Super Bowl in 1970. We suffered another last second loss to Baltimore in that game, but finally went "over the top" in 1971 by beating the Miami Dolphins in the Super Bowl to become

NFL Champions at long last.

Coach Landry's Hall of Fame football record is phenomenal and well documented. However, as I said in the beginning of this chapter, I believe that Tom Landry's human legacy meant more to him than any football legacy. Tom Landry was a true man of character and for me "perseverance" is his number one character trait. He persevered through a humble upbringing in South Texas, he persevered through World War II as a B-17 pilot, and he persevered through a professional football career as both a player and coach. He persevered through the ups and downs of the profession and when that day came when the Dallas Cowboys released him after 29 years, he persevered and never looked back. He persevered through the death of his youngest child, holding fast to the truth of God's Word with faith in his Heavenly Father. And finally, he persevered through his struggle with leukemia and believed that if it was God's timing to call him home, he was ready.

Tom Landry was a teacher. A title of very high calling in my opinion, as our Savior was also often referred to as "Teacher." He was a gracious man, full of integrity, trust and to coin a phrase from NASA and our astronaut program he had the "Right Stuff." Coach Landry treated his players like sons and while he kept a professional distance during your playing days, he would call and encourage you after your playing career ended. He wanted you to be successful in the most important game... "The Game of Life." He led us in prayer before every game. When you played for Coach Landry, you learned about Christ. Not necessarily in a "preachy" way, but by example. He did use and quoted scripture when appropriate. I can safely say that most of his former players were transformed spiritually for the cause of Christ after playing for Coach Landry. We all, and I mean all, cried at his memorial service. He forever remains in the hearts of those who had the privilege and blessing of playing for him. For me, the man from Mission, Texas forever impacted my life. Coach Landry was a man who lived out the "mission" of his Christian faith in hope to honor God and bring people to an understanding of the "Saving Grace" found in a personal relationship with Jesus Christ. His life of faith and perseverance is an example of the great impact we can make, if our life's priorities are in line with God's priorities.

Character Requires Commitment and Perseverance
– Ken Horton

Like Tom Landry, Joseph was a man of great accomplishment, distinguished by innovation and influence. He was also a man who tasted bitter disappointment and yet persevered to impact his family, his closest associates and a nation. Joseph was the eleventh of twelve brothers.[33] His father's special affection for Joseph stimulated a precocious confidence which alienated his brothers and led to a devastating betrayal. After pondering murder, Joseph's brothers chose to sell him to nomads who turned a profit when Potiphar, captain of Pharaoh's guard, bought the young Israelite as a household servant.

Over time Joseph's character and capabilities became obvious to Potiphar. The "Lord was with Joseph,"[34] and Joseph was given responsibility for all of Potiphar's household. Though still a slave, he was now in charge. But he soon became the object of the seductive desires of Potiphar's wife. When he repeatedly refused her advances, declaring his loyalty to both Potiphar and God, she finally grabbed his cloak and falsely claimed that Joseph had molested her. Though Potiphar was angered, he did not have Joseph executed. Instead he was imprisoned, where the warden observed such integrity and perseverance that he made Joseph responsible for all the prisoners. His faithfulness and success gave him the warden's complete confidence.

When the Pharaoh's chief cupbearer and chief baker were imprisoned, Joseph noticed they were dejected. He discovered they had both had dreams. When Joseph heard the dreams, he gave these two officials interpretations anticipating the baker's impending execution and the cupbearer's restoration to his position of significant relationship with the Pharaoh.

Joseph's request that the cupbearer tell Pharaoh about his situation was forgotten and Joseph spent two more years in prison… faithful and effective, but still imprisoned. Finally, the Pharaoh's troubling dream about seven healthy and seven starving cows and seven full and seven shriveled heads of grain jarred the cupbearer's memory. He told Pharaoh about Joseph's ability to interpret dreams. Joseph was summoned and told the Pharaoh that his dream indicated seven years of prosperity followed by seven years of famine. Pharaoh realized that such a dire situation required special leadership by someone "in whom is the spirit of God."[35] In a moment of pivotal insight, Pharaoh gave Joseph the responsibility to prepare the nation for the years ahead as his second-in-command.

What a story of commitment and perseverance! Joseph was betrayed by his brothers, falsely accused by Potiphar's wife, forgotten by the cupbearer, yet he remained faithful to God and was ultimately pivotal in God's purposes. When the famine engulfed the region, Canaan was also afflicted. His father and eleven brothers were desperate for food. So Joseph's brothers came to Egypt seeking food. The rest of the story[36] is full of irony, intrigue and amazing forgiveness. Joseph not only persevered in adversity, but he forgave the brothers who betrayed him and had the joy of being reunited with his father and younger brother, Benjamin.

Joseph's family moved to Egypt, experienced the kindness of Pharaoh because of Joseph, and grew into a great nation. After the death of Jacob, Joseph's brothers feared retribution for their wicked treatment of him. But Joseph modeled the heart of a man whose commitment and perseverance is anchored in confidence in God when he declared, "You intended to harm me, but God intended it for good to accomplish what is now being done, the saving of many lives."[37] It is that kind of rock-solid confidence in God that shapes people of commitment and perseverance... people like Tom Landry... and by God's grace, people like you and me.

Personal Training

1. What have you been most committed to over the last few years? _____, _____, _____.

2. What is the worst thing that has happened in your own life?

3. Why do you think "bad" things happen to "good" people?

4. What does perseverance mean to you?

5. Read II Corinthians 1:3-7. What does this say to you about suffering?

6. Read James 1:2-4. What is the sequence of "outcomes" that result from trials?

7. What new perspectives do you have about persevering through the difficulties of life?

Chapter 6

Character Requires Consistency in Life

If they ever made a Mount Rushmore for sports legends, Tom Landry's visage goes up there first.

The legendary Dallas Cowboys coach was "the Great Stoneface," a living breathing, stoic statute who commanded the Cowboys sideline for twenty-nine years, leading the franchise to 270 victories – third most all-time in the NFL – and appearances in five Super Bowls, two of which they won. On top of that, Landry was a man of principles, virtues and strong Christian faith. The consummate sports role model if there ever was one.

Faith begins with the belief that there is something or someone, greater than oneself. It is to the Christian, a belief in something not seen, in that we "live by faith, not by sight," as it says in II Corinthians 5:7. Landry never hid the fact that he was a man of Christian faith, committed to a God who asks of His followers not to defend Him but to proclaim Him. And that, Landry did. The importance of Landry's faith in this context is not to say that his faith was better or truer than anyone else's. It's to make the point that as successful as he was coaching football and leading men, the sport did not occupy the top spot on his personal ladder of priorities. It was down on a rung somewhere below his love of God and love of family, and that faith never wavered when crowded by worldly success on one side and man's rampant cynicism on the other. Landry stuck to his faith through times when it was unpopular to do so and at other times when it was fashionable to go around wearing it on one's sleeve.

Like most anyone, when I think of Landry, I picture him patrolling the Cowboys sideline, neatly dressed in coat and tie and that ever present fedora. The arms were almost always crossed and there rarely was a smile on his face. There was something honorable, almost old-fashioned, in the manner in which Landry conducted himself as a man coaching a game played by grizzled, grown men with the hearts of exuberant boys. While Landry dressed for football games like most men dressed for church (or at least how men used to dress for church in the era of pre-casual wear), there was never a sense that he thought of games as life-and-death struggles. If he took losses hard, he never really showed it. No throwing his hat. No tearing up yardage markers. No grabbing/yanking of player's faceguards. No berating officials. No gnashing of teeth. Those kinds of things were better left to the Vince Lombardi's and Woody Hayes's of the sport. Then again, there never were any moments of unbridled sideline joy, demonstrated by such acts as jumping into player's arms or racing over to seats and high-fiving fans.

Although my family and I are originally from up-state New York, Landry and the Cowboys had a knack for winning over members of my family. There's my sister Debby, who for some odd reason had long been a Green Bay Packers and Lombardi fan. But all that changed in 1984, when I got tickets for my family to attend the Cowboys-Bills game in Buffalo the Sunday before Thanksgiving. They were excited because they got to sit in the Cowboy's section of the stadium and cheer for Dallas.

I had told Debby that, at the end of the game, she could take her son (my nephew), Scotty, around to where the buses were waiting to take the Cowboys back to the airport. Of course, I couldn't be there with her because of my broadcast duties. With any luck, they would get a chance to see some of the players.

When Debby and Scotty got there, she spotted Tex Schramm, told Scotty who he was, and he got Schramm's autograph. Debby would later tell me how Tex seemed pleased because, as he told her, "Not many people outside of Texas ever ask me for my autograph. It's great to be recognized." Just then, little Scotty spotted Coach Landry and mentioned to his mom, and Debby just told him to be polite and go for it, to ask Coach Landry for his autograph. As Scotty approached the Coach, who was walking swiftly past the fans and trying not to make eye contact with any of them (he must have been disappointed because the Cowboys had just lost the game), Scotty stepped forward and said, "Coach Landry, can I please have your autograph?" Coach Landry leaned over a bit and whispered down to Scotty, "Just keep walking with me."

Debby said "He put his arm around Scotty and guided him in the direction he was walking." When they got to the bus, Coach leaned down to him and asked Scotty his name and then signed the program, and then he immediately stepped onto the bus. As excited as Scotty was in getting Coach Landry's autograph, it made an even greater impression on Debby, because he could have easily brushed off Scotty as he hurried to get on the bus. Until the day she died of breast cancer, there wasn't a bigger Cowboys fan than Debby. This was all because of Coach Landry. He took time to make a difference and put a smile on the faces of a little boy and his mom. Those are the little things that set the Coach apart from so many others.

More than anything else, Landry would be remembered for the character, dignity and grace he brought to the job. The images were emblazoned on our collective consciousness: the coat and tie, the trademark fedora, the crossed arms, the rolled-up game plan, the stone face and stoic demeanor. Tom Landry was a rock, a constant. He also was a man of great faith, a devout Christian who steadily walked a tightrope between proclaiming his faith and cramming it down people's throats. It should surprise no one that he had such an affinity for the Fellowship of Christian Athletes. During the 1980s and 1990s, I often served as emcee at FCA events like the annual FCA Cotton Bowl Breakfast. Because of his involvement at the national level and as Chairman of the Greater Dallas FCA, Coach Landry would regularly be on those programs. These events provided me the opportunity to get to know Tom Landry the person as well as the coach, and I must admit that he's one of the reasons I've stayed involved as a member of the Greater Fort Worth FCA Board for 25-five years. The FCA golf tournament in Dallas that bears his name continues to be one of the most popular and profitable charity events in Texas while "Mr. Cowboy" (Bob Lilly) and I are proud to have just completed our 25th year of the Bob

Lilly – Scott Murray FCA Golf Tournament, benefiting the programs of Greater Fort Worth FCA. Again, our long term commitment is due in great part to Tom Landry, a man who by his very character simply inspired others to give their all and be their best in the most important game we will ever play, the "Game of Life"!

Character Requires Consistency in Life
– Ken Horton

Daniel's life is distinctive, perhaps unique,[38] because the Scripture reveals no character flaws in this young Jewish nobleman. Like all of us, he was not without sin. We simply don't see his frailties in the prophetic book that bears his name. If we are looking for a biblical model of consistency, Daniel is the best the Old Testament offers.

As teenagers Daniel and his three friends are uprooted from their families in Judah and taken as exiles to Babylon. Their nation had been conquered, their lives thrown into chaos,[39] and hundreds of miles from home they had to decide whether they would continue to follow their God. In the face of great pressure they wisely excelled in their studies while courageously following their convictions. Notice they sought permission, suggested solutions and experienced God's blessings.[40] Their behavior illustrated a foundational aspect of consistency: *We do not choose our circumstances, but our choices reveal our character.*

After this strong start, the tests intensified. Nebuchadnez-zar's troubling dream left him so distressed that he requested his wise men to reveal both his dream and the interpretation.[41] In this tough situation, much like a coach developing a game plan without even seeing his opponent, all the wise men balked...except Daniel. When facing this challenge, he sought the support of his friends and the guidance of God.[42] When Daniel correctly revealed the dream and it's meaning to Nebuchadnezzar, he was quick to give God the glory.[43] In this dramatic episode we see a second key to consistency: *When we face life's tests, healthy friendships encourage us to embrace God as our ultimate hope.*

After Daniel's promotion as a key ruler[44] and leader of the wise men, he was apparently in another part of the kingdom when his three friends, Shadrach, Meshach and Abednego, were accused of defying the king because they would not worship the image set up at the prompting of those jealous of the prominence of Daniel and his friends. These three, even in the absence of Daniel, stood boldly for their convictions when threatened with the fiery furnace. Reflect on their response.

> *"16 Shadrach, Meshach and Abednego replied to the king, 'O Nebuchadnezzar, we do not need to defend ourselves before you in this matter. 17 If we are thrown into the blazing furnace, the God we serve is able to save us from it, and he will rescue us from your hand, O king. 18 But even if he does not, we want you to know, O king, that we will not serve your gods or worship the image of gold you have set up.'"* Daniel 3:16-18 NIV

These powerful words indicate a third reality: *Consistency in life is contagious.* It matters who you "hang with." God can use your life to make a lasting difference for others.

God was not only working in the lives of Daniel and his three friends. King Nebuchadnezzar's political success fueled pathological pride. God revealed the consequences of such pride through a dream[45] which Daniel interpreted with clarity and genuine concern for Nebuchadnezzar.[46] The king's stubbornness led to seven years of incapacitation where he lived like an animal.[47] Yet when he recovered and declared his praise of God,[48] his kingdom was still intact. Daniel maintained his loyalty to the king even during his bizarre humiliation. This was perhaps his greatest display of consistency, validating that *loyalty to others was more important than personal advancement.*

Consistency in life… it takes a lifetime to grow toward that pattern.[49] I hope Daniel's life motivates you in the journey.

Personal Training

1. When you get in your car, place the key in the ignition and turn it, what do you expect to happen? When you go to a faucet and turn it, what do you expect to happen? How would you feel, if you never knew the outcome of your car or faucet?

2. Who is the most unreliable person you know? How do you feel when you need that person?

3. Who is the most reliable person you know? How do you feel when you need that person?

4. Read Hebrews 13:5-8. What does this say to you about Jesus Christ?

5. Read Joshua 1:1-5. What did God promise Joshua in verse 5?

6. Do you believe that God is consistently reliable? How can you become more reliable in your relationship with God and others?

Grant Teaff
Executive Director
American Football Coaches Association
Former Head Football Coach
Baylor University

Chapter 7

Character Requires A Sense of Purpose

For over 25 years Coach Tom Landry and I did fundraising for the Fellowship of Christian Athletes. We traveled all over the United States to assist FCA field workers as well as the national office. On several occasions we traveled together on these fundraising events.

Tom Landry was without question the best and most prolific fundraiser in the history of FCA. Coach was admired and loved as the head coach of the Dallas Cowboys, but his work ethic and his passion for the Fellowship of Christian Athletes drove him to give his time and energy to what he believed was the paramount spiritual path for everyone, especially for the youth of America and their coaches.

The FCA's way of fundraising was to saturate a city, community, or even a region with events to tell the story of FCA, and raise funds to support local or area FCA as well as the national initiative.

A normal weekend for those of us who volunteered for FCA would start with travel on a Thursday to somewhere in the United States. Upon arrival, the schedule was full. We would have dinner with field staff and major donors. Friday morning, we would have a minimum of three school assemblies to speak to, while in the afternoon, we would visit an additional three to five athletic departments. We met with the coaching staffs and in many cases the teams. Saturday morning we began with a breakfast with local church ministers. The idea was to make sure that they understood that FCA supported the local churches in their ministry and encouraged young athletes, who had accepted Christ, to join their local churches. Saturday afternoon, we golfed with major donors and potential major donors, then Saturday evening we would have another speaking opportunity at an FCA fundraising dinner. Coaches and athletes locally would give their testimonies. Those in attendance would be asked to consider joining the home teams and donate to assist the FCA field staff in fulfilling their mission. On Sunday mornings, we would speak to at least two church services and then lunch with donors from the churches and those who might have an interest in supporting FCA ministries. Finally, Sunday afternoon we flew home.

Coach Landry and Alicia were asked to host FCA's Tom Landry weekend. Couples from across the nation joined the FCA national staff as well as the regional staff members, depending on where the Landry weekend was held. The FCA story was told in different ways from different individuals and the response was always outstanding.

Not once in all those years, with exhausting fund-raising events did I ever hear Coach Landry complain or say that FCA was taking advantage of him. He cherished the opportunity to serve Christ by being a lightening rod to attract donors.

Watching Coach Landry on and off the field and being around him in different venues, my description of Coach was that he was consistent. He treated everyone with warmth and courtesy. Folks recognized his humble spirit and his Christ-like caring for all who came into his presence.

Coach Landry's physical condition was outstanding. He had forearms and biceps of a strong safety prototype. Those two physical characteristics allowed him to finish each fundraising marathon without slowing down.

Coach Landry was many things to many people. He was the brilliant tough minded coach; the loving father and husband; the Evangelical Christian; the soft spoken speaker with a dynamic message; he was a trusted friend; the heartbeat of the Dallas FCA and nationwide; and of course, he was the "Man in the Hat" to hundreds of thousands of Cowboy fans worldwide. To me Coach Landry was all of the above and more. To me he was the epitome of a man of character.

I once told an audience that in the dictionary there should be a picture of Coach Landry next to the word character. The following is how I define character. Every time I speak or write these words, I see Coach Landry standing on the sidelines.

Success is in the way you walk the paths
of life each and every day,
It's in the little things you do

and in the things you say,
It's not in reaching heights or fame,
It's not in reaching goals,
that all men seek to claim.
Success is being big of heart,
clean, and broad of mind.
Success is being faithful to your friends,
and the stranger, kind.
Success is in your teammates, your family,
and what they learn from you,
Success is having character in everything you do.

In 1980 my Baylor team won the Southwest Conference by three games. We were ranked in the top ten and played in the Cotton Bowl. Having had such a successful year brought a lot of recognition and honor. Two or three weeks after the Cotton Bowl, Donell and I were worshiping in our church in Waco, the First Baptist Church. At the end of the service, we started up the aisle to leave the church, all of a sudden stepping in front of us was a local banker, Bill Nesbit, with his two young boys. Bill, speaking to his boys said, "I want you guys to meet the greatest coach in America." The little redheaded six-year-old stepped right up to me stuck out his hand, loudly and clearly said, "Are you Tom Landry?"

The next time I was with Coach Landry, I told him the story and he absolutely loved it. Every time thereafter, when I was scheduled to introduce him to an audience, he would sidle up to me and ask, "Are you going to tell that story?"

"Yes, I am Coach."

"Good, I sure like that story," with a smile on his face.

On his 70th birthday celebration in Dallas, I was the

emcee, and was scheduled to introduce Coach at the appropriate time during the program. He again sidled up to me and asked if I would tell the story. I, with a smile on my face said, "Oooh, yes." What Coach did not know was that on this occasion, as Paul Harvey would say, I was going to tell "the rest of the story." After telling the audience what the little boy had asked, "Are you Tom Landry?" I concluded with the following:

Donell and Sandra Covington, the wife of Baylor University's team doctor, had driven out to Abilene, Texas, because Donell was going to speak to a gathering of Southern Baptist women, who were there for a convention. During her remarks, Donell told the story of the encounter with Bill Nesbit's son. The audience roared with laughter, but a lady from Mississippi who was sitting next to Donell leaned over to Sandra Covington and said, "Well, everyone knows who Grant Teaff is, but who is that Tom Landry fella?"

Coach Landry laughed even louder when I shared "the rest of the story." His ability to laugh at himself and never take himself too seriously was one of his great characteristics.

Coach Landry's own character was revealed in his personal commitment to his priorities. His relationship to Jesus was paramount. He was always the center of attention because of his fame and instant recognition. Never once, in all our years of friendship did I ever see a personal ego, nor did I ever observe one time where he ever talked down to anyone. He was always kind, considerate, and listened to everyone who approached him.

One year, Coach Landry and I were in Nashville, Tennessee, raising funds for the Fellowship of Christian Athletes when we were asked to appear on a national television program called *Nashville Now*. The host interviewed us for about fifteen minutes concerning our involvement with FCA and at the break, one of the young talents was about three minutes from her debut performance on national television when she came running over to where we were seated and proclaimed how FCA had affected her life in high school and how Coach Landry was such a good Christian example to her and the other young people at her high school. Coach graciously thanked her. Just before she ran off to sing her song she said to the both of us, "I love FCA and I will be happy to sing at any FCA function free of charge." She sang her song and it was evident she was very good. Neither of us knew her name then, but the world knows it now, Faith Hill.

A year after I left coaching to take over the American Football Coaches Association as executive director, I also finished my third book, *Seasons of Glory*. Unbeknownst to me the publisher asked Coach Landry to do the forward for the book. When the book was published and I read his words, I considered it my greatest coaching complement ever–right up there with being elected to the College Football Hall of Fame. Coach Landry said,

> *"I don't know of anyone I have more respect for as a person and as a coach than Grant Teaff. He represents all that is good about coaching. I only wish my son would have had the opportunity to play football under Grant's leadership. When you consider all the struggles and disappointments that we shared as coaches, it is refreshing to see the way Grant can keep every thing in perspective. I am fortunate to be able to call Grant Teaff my friend."*
> *—Tom Landry*

Former Head Football Coach
Dallas Cowboys

Another example of Coach Landry's indomitable character was the way he handled his dismissal as the head coach of the Dallas Cowboys. A nation of admirers looked on and true to his character he was more concerned about his assistant coaches, his players and the staff than he ever was about himself.

In his autobiography, written with Carlton Stowers, when talking about character Coach Landry quoted from Harry Truman's book, *Plain Speaking*, "The *way* in which you endure that which you must endure is more important than the crisis itself."

Coach, later quoted Horace Greeley, who once said, "Fame is a vapor; Popularity is an accident. Riches take wings; Those who cheer today will curse tomorrow; Only one thing endures–character." Coach Landry went on to say, "In my opinion, character is the most important determinant of a person's success, achievement and ability to handle adversity." My latest book, *Grant Teaff with the Master Coaches*, came out of a series of interviews with some of the greatest football coaches of all time.

The Master Coach Series, as it is called, is a live interview each year of two great coaches of the past. Over 11 years I interviewed 22 extremely successful coaches and outstanding leaders in our profession. By asking each of the coaches the same 10 questions, I acquired an accumulation of knowledge unavailable anywhere else–therefore, the book.

The series was an instant hit at the American Football

Coaches Association national convention. Each year over 3,000 coaches attend the hour and a half session. Their joy was to hear these great coaches, in their own words, talk about the most important things in coaching. In 1998, Coach Landry appeared in the Master Coaches Series with Vince Dooley. It was one of the greatest professional coaches teamed with one of the greatest collegiate coaches. As we approached the end of the session, it was time to ask what I consider one of the most important prompts. "Discuss your beliefs about ethics and values."

Coach Landry's answer revealed his deep held belief about his definition of character:

> *"Well, I don't think there's any question about the fact that values and ethics are so important. When we start talking about that, we are talking about character to a large extent. When you have a team with character, then you have a team that is going to be a winner in life–not just on the football field, but in life after they get out of football.*
> *Many of our kids today don't know the difference between right and wrong. That is the difficulty we face across America with our kids right now. My feeling is that we need to continually attack that problem, to help kids feel more and more that they are going to be a part of what life is going to be all about.*
>
> *I think we have a little bit more than just football to talk about, we ought to talk about families today. Hopefully, 1998 will be a special year, when our kids and families have a chance to move forward. The thing I have learned through the years is that family is very important. I see a*

lot of coaches who stay up all night to get ready for games. They don't need to do that. You can do it much easier if you know your wife and your family are there, that you are living this life together as you develop as a coach. I think that is the most important thing today. That's the thing, I feel, the legacy I feel; football should bring players up to a higher level. Whether we can do that, or not, I don't know, but I do know that God can do anything. And when the Lord says He can do something for you, He's going to do it for you and that's the way I feel about football. Football is a great game, but it is not as important as the game of life."

The man in the hat became one of the greatest football coaches of all time, yet the way he lived his life with character, is his greatest legacy.

Character Requires a Sense of Purpose
– Ken Horton

A sense of purpose… how does this key dimension of character develop in the life of a man or woman? We can see it clearly in a Tom Landry or Grant Teaff. But how will it happen in my life?

Nehemiah was a Jewish man who served as the cupbearer[50] for Artaxerxes I during the aftermath of the Babylonian exile.[51] Four realities in his life sharpened his sense of purpose as he was used by God to impact his entire nation.

First, when Nehemiah received the distressing report about conditions in Jerusalem,[52] he saw the personal and spiritual implications of this painful reality with *clarity*. Though he could have avoided these issues, he understood his responsibility to become part of the solution. People with a sense of purpose see their opportunity to make a positive difference and take action.

Nehemiah's first response was prayer and fasting marked by humble confession of his sin and hopeful petition for God's compassionate help.[53] Though this snapshot focuses on only one season of prayer, the immediacy and intimacy of this communion with God suggests a second contribution to Nehemiah's growing sense of purpose: a *consistent pattern of humble prayer*. The God who made us has good works prepared for those who follow Him through faith in Jesus.[54] Time alone with God is essential for an individual to have confidence that his personal sense of purpose reflects God's priorities. Nehemiah finished his time with God with a swelling assurance that his delight in revering God's name positioned him for significant involvement in God's purpose.

It is probable that Nehemiah's mouth was dry and his palms sweaty as he entered the presence of Artaxerxes I. One of the cardinal rules for cupbearers was to display a beaming smile at all times. Kings did not want to be distracted by the problems of their servants. Though Nehemiah attempted to mask his sadness, the king observed his distress. His inquiry struck Nehemiah's heart with fear, because there were numerous cheerful servants waiting to assume his prestigious role. At the risk of his job (and perhaps his life) Nehemiah demonstrated *courage* as he calmly explained his burden for helping rebuild Jerusalem. In the midst of his conversation with Artaxerxes I, Nehemiah "prayed to the God of heaven."[55] His intimacy with God was a continuing reality, giving him wisdom[56] in the midst of this significant moment which established his sense of purpose. Nehemiah boldly requested both permission to return to Jerusalem and provision for the massive rebuilding project. The king's positive response was not based on Nehemiah's compelling presentation, but on God's hand of blessing.[57]

Before Nehemiah arrived in Jerusalem, adversaries were already gathering.[58] As he evaluated the challenge and prepared for the work, the mockery of Sanballat, Tobiah and Geshem only strengthened Nehemiah's conviction that God would provide for their success.[59] As Nehemiah deftly handled the work assignments,[60] the opposition became more vocal[61] and eventually violent.[62] This discouraged some of the workers,[63] but Nehemiah's *confidence* never wavered. Through persistent prayer and encouraging words, he led the people through the turmoil toward completion of the massive rebuilding program.[64]

When there is clarity about the challenge, consistency in humble prayer, courage to risk your comfort for God's purpose and confidence that God will provide for His purposes, people have the *capacity* to finish strong. In fifty-two days of spiritual dependence and proactive work, the walls of Jerusalem were rebuilt.

The presence of physical walls did not eliminate adversaries or thorny challenges in leading the people. But God's work through Nehemiah anchored a sense of purpose in his life that established him as a model leader.

Personal Training

1. Have you ever seriously thought about your purpose in life?

2. What has guided or motivated your life to date (i.e., materialism, career, comfort, status)?

3. Do you find yourself becoming "bored" or unfulfilled with life?

4. Read Genesis 1:26-31. Did God create man to have a specific purpose? What was that purpose?

5. How do you think your life would be enriched if you understood God's purpose for your life?

6. Read the book "Purpose Driven Life" by Rick Warren. Warren clearly explains God's five purposes for each of us:

- We were planned for God's pleasure, so your first purpose is to offer real worship.

- We were formed for God's family, so your second purpose is to enjoy real fellowship.

- We were created to become like Christ, so your third purpose is to learn real discipleship.

- We were shaped for serving God, so your fourth purpose is to practice real ministry.

Kyle Rote, Jr.
Former Professional Soccer Player
3 Time Winner of ABC Television's
Superstars Competition

Chapter 8

Character Requires
Authentic Personal Evaluation

It was the end to a most remarkable Sunday—December 30th 1956 – a day that many football historians consider a defining moment for a team, a city and the future of the National Football League.

Just a few hours earlier the New York Giants had won the World Championship beating the favored George Halas led Chicago Bears by a shocking score of 47-7. The city of New York prepared to embrace their team with a championship parade. The NFL began to seriously explore the idea of expanded national television for a league that finally moved from regional popularity in blue-collar towns to an era when cosmopolitan cities like Chicago, Los Angeles and New York joined the fan base. Indeed, within just two years of this game the NY Giants had the largest group of season ticket holders for any sporting team in the world. Now the mill and coal industrial revolution centers like Pittsburgh, Cleveland, Baltimore, and Detroit were put on notice that the Giants were no longer an easy team to play. Indeed, for the ten-year period from 1954-1963 the Giants would never finish lower than 3rd place.

That night every member of our Giant's family celebrated . . . with only one exception. The fans were ecstatic as the game wasn't even close. We watched the owners, the Mara's, the equipment man, Sid Moret, and even the casual New Yorker on the street identify with the "world champs." It didn't matter what kind of collar you wore – you shouted in unison " Deee – fense" during games as the Giants were now everyman's team. Indeed, income I received from Autographs that I sold on the streets of the Bronx soared! Autographs from Frank Gifford, Pat Summerall, Charlie Conerly, and Sam Huff among others including my father Kyle Rote were now being sold and traded for about double what they were just a few days before (from 5 cents to 10 cents) The love affair continues to this day with a waiting list for season tickets now requiring a wait of approximately 23 years.

However, beyond the public fanfare of the dramatic changes occurring in the NFL, the city of New York, and the Giants organization – another more personal change was about to occur to the only man in the Giants organization who found the Giants' world championship a personal disaster . . . Tom Landry.

Tom had retired as a player a year earlier after the 1955 season as a heralded defensive player/coach. The year 1956 was the first year he spent 100 percent of his time coaching and refining the umbrella defense. Indeed, he was the man most responsible for totally shutting down the Bears potent offense. This coaching dominance in holding the Bears to just 7 points created what he would later call "the worst day of his life." Why?

Over the years I have heard the story of this "Day of Victory" several times from Coach Landry – but the important thing is to recognize that his story is in many ways – your story . . . and my story. Oh, the details of his story are likely quite different – there are not many World War II B-17 pilots left who flew 30 missions over Germany nor have many of us ever visited Coach's hometown of Mission Texas let alone lived there. But, I dare say all of us have tried to fill the "God shaped" hole in each of our hearts with athletic, business, social, monetary or even military success. . . . Coach Landry had as well, starting in high school when he was sure that achieving an undefeated football season would give him "satisfaction." It didn't – so he then set his sights on succeeding in college football – he did, but it didn't satisfy him either. Then, piloting a bomber and surviving a crash landing, same result. Finally, he realized that satisfaction could only come from one last place – pro football. So he competed for years and achieved star status as a player and then finally on this December 30th 1956 night in his first year as a full time Coach—his world collapsed.

Coach Landry, in his early 30's, had done it all—a decorated war vet, an all-pro caliber player, and now with the days events, he was also a successful, world champ coach. It couldn't get any better . . . but it also couldn't get any worse. With great regret he spent that night pondering the years he wasted. That remarkable athletic resume for success he had achieved still didn't satisfy. Even a world championship didn't fill that God-shaped hole in his heart. So, while the rest of us rejoiced in a team world championship – Tom reflected on his individual world disaster.

He thought back about how he had spent his whole life trying to climb mountain after mountain to achieve personal satisfaction. In football there were no more mountains to climb. There were no more missions to fly. He had been to football's Mt. Everest—a World Championship—and it still wasn't enough.

That memorable day in NFL history was a culmination of a sporting dream for everyone associated with the Giants, except one. For Coach Landry that day was just the beginning of his faith journey to the foot of the Cross. The rugged, stone faced man who many of us saw as a champion of self-control "died to self" and began to look beyond his own efforts to the sacrificial love of Jesus Christ. He became a "Champion of God control" – His heart began to fill in—not because he had a "ring" –but because he now had Christ His trading card became pricey for a while. His life had become priceless forever. Now that's a defining moment.

Character Requires
Authentic Personal Evaluation
– Ken Horton

When Tom Landry took an audit of his life and discovered spiritual bankruptcy, he joined an ever-expanding circle of people who have looked beyond themselves to a Savior offering a treasure that cannot be earned, but must be accepted by humble faith.

The Apostle Paul would have understood Landry's journey. When Paul stacked up his accomplishment he was as much an All-Pro in the religious realm as Tom Landry was in athletics. His Jewish pedigree was impeccable, having accomplished everything expected of him and then some. He was a Pharisee among the elite in Israel's social order.[65] He had outdistanced his contemporaries in his furious zeal to eliminate a rival religious movement known popularly as *The Way*.[66] He devoted himself to observing the requirements of the Mosaic Law, reaping the personal and relational benefits of that system.

But it was not enough. Using the language of an accountant, Paul placed his life on a balance sheet and tallied his liabilities and assets. All of his personal and religious accomplishments ended up in the loss column, like rubbish.[67] Only one reality remained in the gain column... the privilege of knowing Jesus Christ personally through faith. The righteousness which had eluded him through his exhaustive religious effort had become his blessing through faith in Jesus.[68]

Now his focus was on knowing Christ, experiencing His resurrection power, sharing in His sufferings, and becoming like Him in sacrificial love for others.[69]

Like Paul, Tom Landry's personal evaluation reshaped his focus and transformed his life. Instead of obsessing about past wins and losses, the guiding principle of life became a passion to please Jesus.[70] This released Coach Landry to respond to life in a way that stimulated the spiritual curiosity of others. When they began to probe, they discovered that facing your spiritual bankruptcy is the pivotal step in receiving God's indescribable gift, Jesus Christ.[71]

Personal Training

1. "Authentic Evaluation" separates the great coaches from the good coaches. What do you think that statement means?

2. "Authentic Evaluation" means you have the courage to examine every area with an open mind based on the reality of the situation or circumstances. Why would this be a good character quality for personal life application?

3. Read Matthew 19:16-22. Do you think the "Rich Young Ruler" had the courage to authentically evaluate the core being of his life? What controlled the Rich Young Ruler's heart?

4. Take an authentic personal inventory of every area of your life. Marriage, family, career, habits, physical fitness. With courage and an open mind based on the reality of the circumstances, what areas need immediate corrective attention?

5. Now take an authentic personal inventory of your spiritual fitness. What is controlling your heart and keeping you from experiencing God's full measure of love in your life? What are you going to do about it?

Dal Shealy
Former FCA National President
and College Football Coach

Chapter 9

Character Requires A Servant's Heart

I first began to follow the success and progress of Coach Tom Landry when I was coaching football in the early 1970's at Carson-Newman College in east Tennessee. We had been watching the Dallas Cowboys football team and our family became BIG Cowboy fans and fans of Coach Landry. We had been involved in the Fellowship of Christian Athletes and knew of Coach and his involvement in FCA. Therefore, we believed we had a two-way connection and spirit with Coach Landry and the Cowboys.

After four years of leading the Carson-Newman College Eagles and playing for the NAIA National Championship, we moved to Baylor University in Waco, Texas. I had the blessing of coaching with Coach Grant Teaff, and being in Texas, where I could easily visit with the Cowboys and met and talked with Coach Landry. He was always very nice and gave me an open door to visit most any time I could. We won the

Southwest Conference Championship for the first time in 50 years, and played in the Cotton Bowl for the first time ever. Coach Teaff was selected by the American Football Coaches Association, and was the Head Coach for the All-American Bowl game. He asked me to draft the west team for the AA Bowl and coach the offense. So I contacted Coach Landry and he and Gil Brandt were great about giving me the scoop on a number of student-athletes for our consideration and selection for the game.

Therefore, I knew Coach Landry from the standpoint of a football coach and enjoyed going and watching his Cowboys practice, etc. Even though he was very busy as the head coach, he was always open to visit and make me feel special. So he became one of my heroes, and a mentor in football, scouting and coaching the offense and defense. He served as his own coordinator on both sides of the ball for a number of years.

Following 27 years of coaching and being a volunteer for the Fellowship of Christian Athletes working their camps, serving on the local and state boards and being the Huddle leader wherever I coached during those years, I left the University of Richmond in Virginia as head coach to move to Kansas City, MO and work for FCA.

During my tenure in Kansas City with FCA, I had the honor of working closely with Coach Landry where he served as a Trustee, and later as a Lifetime Trustee of FCA. We also had a Tom Landry Weekend for our major donors, their spouses and FCA staff and Board of Trustees. We held these events at different locations during football season. Coach and Mrs. Alicia Landry would meet with us, and he usually spoke to everyone on Friday evening. We would have other speakers, the Board would meet and the folks would all attend the Cowboy game on Sunday after a morning Worship service. Coach also served as the Chairman of the Greater Dallas FCA Board and led the ministry effort with our Dallas area staff. During his leadership days, Dallas had the greatest impact and largest ministry in the nation.

Tom Landry would willingly go anywhere and speak on behalf of the FCA ministry and helped raise funding for staff and events all over the USA. After Coach Landry left the Cowboys, he and Alicia would continue to host the Tom Landry Weekends, and other special occasions. Coach would travel all over the country and it was my honor and blessing to travel with him many times. He had a great sense of humor and a great laugh which you would not expect after watching him work on the sidelines during football games. He was so focused and was known by his trademark hat. Many times he would sign a hat and let us auction it off at a FCA luncheon or banquet. We raised a lot of support for FCA staff by the hats and balls he signed and we auctioned.

One time in Arizona at a fund raising banquet, we had a football he had autographed that we were auctioning. The bid got up to $10,000. Two men were bidding for the ball. John O'Dell, the FCA Regional Director, stopped the auction and asked if they would both pay ten thousand for a ball, they answered yes, so Coach Landry autographed another ball and FCA had a great $20,000 reward.

Another trip I made up to the northwest to work with our Oregon Director, Joe Broeker, resulted in a very interesting visit with a potential major donor. We went to his office to ask him to make a very large gift to the FCA in Oregon. As we walked into his office waiting area, we observed several glass display cases with some outstanding items he had collected. As we visited with the potential donor, we asked him for a very large gift. He said that he'd give us the gift if we could get him a football signed by Coach Tom Landry and his quarterback Roger Staubach. I called Coach and shared with him our need. He said he'd take care of it and get a ball that he and Roger would sign. He wanted to know where to send the ball, so we gave him Joe's address. About a week later Joe received the ball, took it to the potential donor and picked up a check in the amount of $75,000 from the donor.

We had many trips together for FCA. I'll never forget the time we were to share at a fundraising dinner in Fort Lauderdale, FL. I arrived at the airport first and met our FCA staff person. We then went to the gate where Coach's plane was to arrive. When he came through the door, people began to gather around him seeking autographs. I told Coach Landry that the mayor of Ft. Lauderdale had a press conference planned on the canal and they were placing a concrete square, three feet by three feet, with a Dallas Cowboy Star set in it. They wanted Coach Landry to sign his name and put his hand prints in the concrete. We were running tight on time, but Coach kept walking and signing anyone's paper, book, etc. for them. He was very kind and did not want to turn anyone away or disappoint them. We made the mayor's event and press conference on time. Afterward went to the hotel to change clothes and rest prior to the dinner. There were folks who somehow found out where we were staying and were waiting for him to get there in order to get pictures and autographs. I think he must have signed at least thirty or forty before we could get him to his room. Coach Landry laughed and said, *"I can't believe these people would still want my autograph since I've been out of football all these years."*

In 2002 we finished building the new Home Office Service Center for the Fellowship of Christian Athletes and had the dedication in August of that year. One of the highlights was the dedication of the Coach Tom Landry Worship Center. We had some of his personal items that Mrs. Alicia Landry and son Tom Jr. donated in a glass display case. Also, famed western artist, Jack White painted a life size oil of Coach holding a game plan during one of the Super Bowls. The picture White used for the painting did not show a good view of Coach Landry's hand. One day Coach Grant Teaff was visiting with White and he used Teaff's hand as a model for the painting. This is truly fitting, since Coach meant so much to Grant and had a great impact on his life.

I guess my most memorable time with Coach Landry was during one of our last trips together for the Fellowship of Christian Athletes. We ended up having to room together due to lack of rooms at the hotel we were staying. Coach just relaxed and shared a lot about his life, philosophy of coaching, his coming to Christ and the importance that God had in his life. We laughed and shared for several hours. He greatly impacted my life and gave me a night I'll never forget.

I loved the man, the coach, the husband, the father and friend in Christ. I was blessed to have known Coach Tom Landry, and to have had some of my greatest life memories.

Character Requires a Servant's Heart
– Ken Horton

Joseph was a Levite from the Jewish tribe responsible for the worship at the Temple. His family had migrated to Cyprus, perhaps during one of the numerous assaults on Israel which occurred during the centuries before Jesus was born. As his family prospered on this beautiful Mediterranean island, Joseph apparently maintained his engagement with the religious practices of Judaism. When he heard about Jesus (or perhaps met him personally) Joseph embraced Him as the promised Messiah and became part of the expanding community of believers in Jesus who remained in Jerusalem after Jesus' ascension.

Since many were pilgrims who had trusted Christ at Pentecost and the weeks afterward,[72] there were unusual financial needs associated with assimilating these thousands of people. Joseph is introduced in the pages of Scripture as an example of exceptional kindness,[73] selling a piece of property and giving all the proceeds to support people with financial needs. Spontaneously he illustrated a distinctive trait of servanthood: *joyful generosity.*

During those early years, a Pharisee named Saul became a vicious persecutor of the followers of Jesus. After he was transformed on the road to Damascus,[74] he was not embraced by many who had been scarred by his assaults. It was Joseph who welcomed him to Jerusalem and endorsed his ministry in Antioch,[75] exhibiting a second characteristic of a servant's heart: *encouraging affirmation.*

Years later Joseph was sent to Antioch by the church in Jerusalem to encourage the growing community of believers there.[76] When he realized he needed help, he recruited Saul from his hometown of Tarsus[77] and together they helped this church become the launch point for missions to the Gentile world. It is not surprising that Joseph and Saul were chosen to lead that strategic effort.[78] As they made their way through Cyprus, Joseph's home territory, Joseph was the leader. But by the time Saul had become known as Paul[79] and they arrived on the coast of Pamphylia (southern Turkey today), Paul was more prominent, the key spokesman for the good news about Jesus. Some would have been offended, but Joseph remained a faithful partner in God's purposes, modeling a third distinctive of a servant's heart: *consistent humility.*

Paul and Joseph did eventually part ways. They had a sharp disagreement[80] on whether to give Mark, who had abandoned them on their first journey,[81] a second chance. Joseph insisted that his young cousin would become a fruitful representative of Jesus. Paul knew that he was not the one to help him in that direction. So Paul and Silas went back to southern Turkey and Joseph and Mark went to Cyprus. We hear almost nothing about Joseph after this point, but we do know that his investment in Mark had lasting value. At the end of Paul's life he asks Timothy to bring Mark to Rome "because he is helpful to me in my ministry."[82]

Mark later wrote a Gospel with a distinctive focus on presenting the story of Jesus to Gentile readers. Through his loyal friendship to Mark, Joseph demonstrated the *enduring loyalty* anchored in a servant's heart.

Sometimes nicknames tell us a lot about a person. Joseph's friends gave him one: Barnabas, which means *son of encouragement.*[83] May we join his tribe!

Personal Training

1. Oswald Chambers said, *"Service is the overflow of a life filled with love and devotion."* What is the message our present culture sends about "service"?

2. Can you think of a time when someone graciously served you and you could tell it brought joy to them? How did that act of service make you feel?

3. Read Luke 10:38-40. Does Martha's view of service resemble yours or someone you know? What about those family holiday times?

4. Read Matthew 20:20-28. Jesus said, "Just as the Son of Man did not come to be served, but to serve, and to give His life a ransom for many."

5. What new insights on "serving" have you gained? Are you willing to readjust your life and priorities to "serving"?

Chapter 10

The Final Word

Growing up in Dallas, Texas in the early 1960's, I was introduced to team sports by my grandmother, who was a big sports fan. She actually took me to my first youth league baseball tryout when I was nine-years-old. She also took me to my first Dallas Cowboys football game in 1966 at the Cotton Bowl. It would be the first of many trips there that my friends and I would make. One dollar would get you in the game and as young kids; those end-zone seats at the Cotton Bowl were just fine for us. I guess my admiration for Tom Landry began as I sat in that end zone and watched "Dandy" Don Meredith launch those "bombs" to "Bullet" Bob Hayes.

I had learned how to play ball at school and on the streets of my neighborhood with some of the older kids. I actually got "cut" from that first team I tried out for, but I did not even know what that meant. There was a coach from another team there and he told all the boys that were cut, that they could tryout for his team, which I made and my baseball career was off and running so to speak.

One of those older kids in the neighborhood happened to be a high school athlete named Donnie Young. I was mesmerized by Donnie Young. Not only did we have the same first name, we had the same birthday, August 11th. Donnie had a neighborhood friend named Gil Wilokie and they did all of the things guys did back then. Their friendship and the things they did might have been a little bit like a scene out of the old television show, "Leave it to Beaver." Those of you over 45-years-old know what I am talking about. Donnie and Gil had actually built a go-cart when they were in junior high school (I'm sure their dads helped them). You could not imagine how happy and surprised I was, when on my 11th birthday, Donnie and Gil gave me that go-cart as a birthday present. That go-cart did have a downside, however. It had no brakes. You had to "kill" the engine and then pull on a piece of lumber attached to the side to drag on the ground to slow the cart to a stop. That proved to be a tricky endeavor at times. Donnie Young played high school football and baseball. Young took an interest in me. He threw the football with me, taught me how to field a baseball and simply made time for me. Young was a running back and punter on his high school football team and that same year he taught me how to punt the football. When I tried out for my first "pee wee" football team, the coaches asked the boys who could kick the football. About a half dozen boys raised their hands including me. Being one of the smaller boys at the time, I am sure they did not think I could punt the ball very far or very good. Well, I instantly made the team when I stepped up there and booted a perfect spiral punt. They were shocked, because not many 11-year-old kids could kick a spiral punt.

Donnie Young wore button down collar shirts that were neatly ironed with penny loafer shoes. He was the classic "All-American" guy. Donnie drove a 1959 Chevy Impala convertible, and yes, he and his friend Gil would let me pile in the back seat occasionally and off we would go, cruising to the drive-in to get a Coke. Donnie would always introduce me to his teenage friends, both boys and girls. Donnie had a ping-pong table in his garage and in the summers when he got off from his summer job, the garage door would open up and I would join him and Gil with a few other kids and we played ping-pong for hours on end.

Well guess what, because of Donnie Young, Donnie Snyder wore button down collar shirts and penny loafer shoes. My Mom was surprised when I wanted to iron my shirts, but she actually taught me how and at age ten, I would iron my shirts, because I wanted to be just like Donnie Young. I bought a convertible when I was in college, probably because I so loved those times that Donnie Young drove me around with that top down.

Donnie Young graduated high school and my family moved across town. I have no idea whatsoever about Young's Christian faith. I don't ever remember him talking about God and don't know if he was a Christian. All I can tell you is that Donnie Young had a huge *influence* on me. He took more interest in me than anyone else in my life at that time, including my father. By the grace of God, I am thankful that his influence was very positive and I would love to talk to him today, but I have no idea where he is or if he is even living.

"Influence," is one of the founding principles of the Fellowship of Christian Athletes. Everyone has a sphere of influence. Tom Landry said that, other than his father, his high school football coach had the greatest influence on his life.

Committed to pursuing a vision that God had given him to capitalize on "influence" and the platform of sports to share the Gospel of Jesus Christ, Don McClanen set out on what probably seemed an impossible mission for a young college

basketball coach at a very small school in Eastern Oklahoma.
The idea of using sports and sports celebrities to share
Christ with people came to him in the late 1940's. Through
perseverance, Don McClanen saw that early vision become a
reality when in 1954 the Fellowship of Christian Athletes was
born.

In chapter 9, we discussed *"authentic evaluation."* Remember *"authentic evaluation"* means you have the courage to
examine every area with an open mind based on the reality of
the situation or circumstances. The truly great coaches don't
fear authentic evaluation, because they can then begin the
corrective measures necessary to improve. Well, if we are
authentic about our present culture, we would come to grips
with the fact that we live in a very "dark culture." Oh, it may
not look like it on the surface, but if you barely scratch away
at the surface, a dark reality exists. For instance, for everything
good about the Internet, there are at least 100 things bad. We
are grossly naïve if we don't believe that teenagers are looking
at pornography on the web and that it is not having a negative effect on their self esteem and future relationships. If we
are honest, we all have to admit that everyone is just a few
"mouse clicks" away from being where they should not be.
Television ads are being run today by pharmaceutical companies that say 20 percent of adults have genital herpes. Is there
a correlation? You make the call.

What about "Sanctity of Life"? I happen to be "pro-life,"
but I don't care where you are on this issue, when over one
million abortions are being performed annually, we need to
be authentic and recognize that it has become another form
of birth control. What does that say about our culture?
"Sanctity of Life" goes much farther. Gang violence and

armed robberies consistently end in human death. People are killed by gang members as initiation into the gang. Criminals are killing people for small amounts of cash or property. Human cloning, assisted suicide and euthanasia bring on other major ramifications about where our culture stands on the value of human life. The Bible says *"And the Lord God formed man out of the dust of the ground, and breathed into his nostrils the breath of life; and man became a living being" (Genesis 2:7 NKJ)*. A holy and righteous God literally "breathes," His breath of life into His creation and we destroy it as if it has no value. I could go on, but make no mistake, we live in a "dark culture"

The good news is; *"In the beginning, God created the heavens and the earth. The earth was without form, and void; and darkness was on the face of the deep. And the Spirit of God was hovering over the face of the waters. Then God said, let there be light; and there was light" (Genesis 1:1-3 NKJ)*. This light was not the Sun, as that is created later. This light is a special divine light, created by God to eliminate the darkness. You see God created light to eliminate darkness. Not the other way around. Light always eliminates darkness. I find it interesting that some 2,000 years ago, God brought another divine light into the world to eliminate darkness, the "Light of Jesus Christ!"

Did you know that the Bible mentions the word "heart" over 700 times? Most of the time it is mentioned it means "the innermost being." God must be pretty interested in our innermost being. In essence, the innermost being is what this book on Tom Landry's character has been all about. Our character is a derived from our innermost being. I submit that God wants our hearts above all else. The scriptures are full of examples of God working on the hearts of people like, Abraham, Jacob, Moses, David, Peter and Paul to name a few. Why? Because when God has your heart, He has you!

I don't know about you, but I do not believe that our present culture is what our Founding Fathers had in mind. The historical record indicates that the vast majority were Christian, intently Christian. If they could have fast forwarded to today, they would be greatly disappointed at how our free society has corrupted their vision of *"life, liberty and the pursuit of happiness."* Yes, they were fallible and imperfect, but they set forth a government intended to be based on the inalienable rights given to all mankind by of our Creator. Nothing like it had existed before. While one might argue it took too long, over time, this government allowed for true inclusiveness of race and gender.

The Founding Fathers knew you could not legislate morality and that a free society had to rely on the church as a "check" on the culture of each generation. John Adams said, *"Our Constitution was made only for a moral and religious people. It is wholly inadequate to the government of any other."* In the last half of the 20th century an *"all out"* assault was levied on this free society government and the Constitution intended for a "moral and religious people" as described by John Adams has been manipulated and perverted at times to provide rights to an immoral few, thus leaving the door wide open to moral and cultural decline.

Furthermore, I don't believe our present culture is what those men were fighting for at Omaha Beach on D-Day. I don't believe it is what our men were fighting for on Iwo Jima and I don't believe it is what Tom Landry was fighting for when he had to crash-land that B-17 in World War II.

I am a strong believer in this country and the political

process we have here in America. While not perfect, it has been the most unique form of government and self-determination ever created in the history of the world. I am also a strong believer in social services and humanitarian work, as this models the earthly ministry of Christ. We have a misplaced hope however, if we believe these will change the culture with any real substance. You see the hope for our culture and therefore the hope for America will not be found in any politician or political process. The hope for our culture and the hope for America will not be found in any social advocate or social services. The hope for America will only be found in a people with changed hearts. When the innermost being is changed, lives are changed and a person's worldview changes. Therefore, the true hope for America will only be found in one place, and that place is the person of Jesus Christ. The hope for America will only be found in Jesus Christ because only Jesus Christ can change the heart, the innermost being of a person. If we want to change the American culture, we must be about reaching America with that second divine light God brought into the world, the Light of Jesus Christ. Remember light was created to eliminate darkness, not the other way around.

Over the years since 1954, the FCA ministry model and concept began to penetrate the athletic community throughout America and eventually people from all walks of life saw the incredible effectiveness of the ministry in presenting the message of Christ to people of all ages but especially the youth of America. From its birth to present day, the Fellowship of Christian Athletes has first and foremost been committed to "evangelism," sharing the truth about what it means to have a faith relationship with Jesus Christ and the hope that brings for this life and life eternal.

I believe that FCA is strategically positioned in this present culture to reach teenagers with the Gospel of Jesus Christ, now like never before. The two greatest cultural influencers of youth today are sports and music, bar none.

The platform of sports is unbelievable in our culture and growing every year. The spectrum of sports continues to grow as well. Have you ever been to a NASCAR event for example? Many times there are over 200,000 people at these events. There are teenagers walking the halls of our schools who are great athletes and sports enthusiasts that don't play on the traditional school sports teams. They participate in Motocross, high level club sports, martial arts, etc. All under this cultural phenomenon called "sports."

Additionally, when Title IX was enacted in 1973, it required that public schools had to offer the same amount of sports opportunities for girls as it did boys. The FCA target audience immediately doubled with this legislation as girl's sports sky-rocketed throughout our country.

Now, think about the leadership teams of Fortune 500 companies in America. I'm not just talking about the top two or three executives. Take a look at the top ten people in those companies and I guarantee a good percentage of them have some sort of athletic background. These companies don't talk about managing people today, they talk about "coaching" people. Organizationally, they refer to "teams" rather than departments. These companies seek to motivate their employees and implement goal setting strategies from America's top coaches. If we reach these leaders for Christ through sports when they are young, what type of decisions do you think will begin to be made in the boardroom? Ethics will begin to replace greed. Employees will be valued again and philanthropy to Christ-centered endeavors will increase, just to name a few.

Finally, FCA is strategically positioned to reach the youth of America today because of one basic but critical element… coaches. The middle school, high school and college coaches of America have a huge influence on the youth in their schools. Coaches are the most influential faculty members on the school campus. I am not saying that other faculty members don't have influence. Coaches simply are the most influential. Their influence goes beyond their teams into the entire student body. Almost every kid knows who the coaches are in their school. I bet you remember your coaches. As a former coach myself, I could get my athletes to do things their parents could never get them to do. I could influence their study habits, their social habits and even their personal appearance, all because I was their coach.

From the very beginning, FCA has worked with coaches to capitalize on their influence in the schools. They literally become "built-in" extensions of the FCA staff on a campus and are the main reason the FCA is so effective from a ministry standpoint and cost standpoint. Coach Landry used to say that FCA is the "best bang for the buck" in America. He would tell people that if they would invest financially in FCA and did not like the results, he would give them their money back.

FCA works with coaches on all levels. Every major coaching function in America has an FCA presence there. Organizations like the American Football Coaches Association (AFCA) and the Texas High School Coaches Association (THSCA) have FCA booths and FCA Coaches Breakfast as a part of their annual conventions for example. Walking into the AFCA – FCA breakfast each year is like walking into the "who's who" of major college football. It is not unusual to see the likes of Bobby Bowden, Jim Tressel, Tom Osborne or Mark Richt. These coaches have been personally touched by the FCA ministry and understand the effectiveness it has to reach young people with the Gospel.

The Fellowship of Christian Athletes ministry model has evolved to reach just about anyone who has interest in sports, any sport. The FCA Ministries encourage, equip and empower coaches and athletes on the professional, college, high school, junior high and youth levels to use the powerful medium of sports to impact their world for Jesus Christ. The FCA Ministries are: Coaches Ministry, Campus Ministry, Camp Ministry and Community Ministry.

Today, FCA is the largest youth ministry of its kind in America. In 2008, FCA directly touched over two million lives and the influence is growing everyday. From one man, Don McClanen, to over 900 staff today, FCA is literally positioned to be the "point of the spear" when it comes to youth evangelism in our country. You can be involved in this powerful outreach by plugging-in to FCA in your local community. All you have to do is go to www.fca.org to learn more about being on Team FCA. Remember, if you want to change the culture, you are going to have to change some hearts. Only Jesus Christ can change a heart. If we don't share the "Light" of Christ, darkness will continue to prevail. If not us, then who? If not now, then when? Check out FCA's website www.morethanwinning.org.

FCA Ministry Components

(Source: Fellowship of Christian Athletes)

Coaches Ministry

At the heart of FCA are coaches. Our role is to minister to them by encouraging and equipping them to know and serve Christ. FCA ministers to coaches through Bible studies, staff contacts, prayer support, discipleship and mentoring, Behind the Bench (a program for coaches wives), resources, outreach events, national and local conventions, conferences and retreats.

Campus Ministry

The Campus Ministry is initiated and led by student-athletes and coaches on junior high, high school and college campuses. The programs of the Campus Ministry include Huddles, Team Bible Studies, Chapel Program, Team FCA Membership, One Way 2 Play – Drug Free! and Special Events.

Camp Ministry

Camps are a time of "inspiration and perspiration" for athletes and coaches to reach their potential by offering comprehensive athletic, spiritual and leadership training. The types of Camps are Sports Camp, Leadership Camp, Coaches Camp, Youth Sports Camp and Partnership Camp.

Community Ministry

The non-school based FCA ministries reach the community through partnerships with the local churches, businesses, parents and volunteers. These ministries not only reach out to the community, but also allow the community to invest in athletes and coaches. Community Ministries include: Stewardship Ministries, Adult Ministries, Sport-Specific Ministries, Membership, Urban Initiatives, Global Sports Development, Clinics, Product and Resource Development, and Professional Athlete Ministries.

FCA Ministry Distinctives

- Christ Centered—focus of our message
- Kingdom Minded—serving the purpose of the Church
- Bible Based—source of our authority
- Athletically Focused—ministering to coaches and athletes
- Spiritually Nurturing—helping people to know and grow in Christ
- Fellowship Oriented—connecting people through the love of Christ
- Volunteer Intensive—mobilizing adults to accomplish the mission
- Culturally Adaptive—meeting the diverse needs of people
- Faith Financed—funded through people moved by God to give

FCA's Statement of Faith

We believe the Bible to be the inspired, the only infallible, authoritative Word of God. (2 Timothy 3:16-17; 2 Peter 1:20-21)

We believe that there is only one God, eternally existent in three persons: Father, Son and Holy Spirit. (1 Peter 1:1; Matthew 28:19)
We believe in the deity of Christ, in His virgin birth, in His

sinless life, in His miracles, in His vicarious and atoning death through His shed blood, in His bodily resurrection, in His ascension to the right hand of the Father, and in His personal return in power and glory. (Deity-John 1:1, 14) (Atonement-Hebrews 9:15-22) (Virgin Birth-Matthew 1:18, 25) (Bodily Resurrection-1 Corinthians 15:1-4) (Sinless Life-Hebrews 4:15) (Personal Return-Hebrews 9: 27-28)

We believe that for the salvation of lost and sinful men (women) regeneration by the Holy Spirit is absolutely essential. (John 3:3, 16; John 5:24; Titus 3: 3-7)

We believe in the present ministry of the Holy Spirit, by whose indwelling the Christian is enabled to live a godly life. (John 14: 15-26; John 16: 5-16; Ephesians 1:14)

We believe in the resurrection of both the saved and the lost, they that are saved unto the resurrection of life and they that are lost unto the resurrection of damnation. (Romans 6:23; 1 John 5:12; Matthew 13:41-43 Matthew 25:31-46)

We believe in the spiritual unity of believers in our Lord Jesus Christ. (Philippians 2: 1-2)

Additional FCA Information

According to one source, 96% of all Americans participate in or watch an athletic event every week. FCA has chosen the powerful medium of athletics as its avenue to impact the world for Christ. Specifically, FCA has targeted the athlete and coach because of their great influence.

In his book, *The Coming Revolution in Youth Ministry,* published in 1992 by Victor Books, Mark Senter III, Ph.D., analyzes the structure of several youth ministries and their method for accomplishing their purpose and mission. Dr. Senter writes,

"At the end of the decade of the 1980's, FCA had regular contact with students on more campuses than the next three largest parachurch youth ministries combined. The strength of the organization (FCA) is a dedicated core of volunteer Huddle groups leaders who invest their spare time. The linkage is a natural one. Coaches, or people connected with high school athletic programs, invite male and female athletes to participate in group meetings where the language of sports is mixed with the Word of God. The organization (FCA) did not need to be highly visible in order to pay staff members to work on a particular campus because a willing worker was already in place."

A survey of the nation's junior and senior high schools by the Southern Baptist Convention Data Bank, found that FCA is on more campuses, reaching more students on a weekly basis than all other Christian organizations combined (March 1995 findings).

God gave Don McClanen, one man, a vision for impacting his country for the cause of Christ by using the highly influential platform of sports. Since 1954, the Fellowship of Christian Athletes has been doing just that. My prayer is that you will catch the "Vision of Influence" and join Team FCA in your community. All you have to do is visit the FCA website at www.fca.org to learn how you can make an eternal impact right in your own community.

Notes

[1] Romans 4:1-25; Hebrews 11:8-19

[2] Located in modern Iraq

[3] Located in modern Turkey

[4] Because his wife, Sarah, was so beautiful, Abraham feared for his life. Two times (Genesis 12:10-20; 20:1-18) Abraham claimed Sarah was his sister, putting her and their marriage in grave peril.

[5] Numbers 13:1-25

[6] Numbers 13:26

[7] Numbers 13:33

[8] Numbers 14:1-9

[9] Numbers 14:20-23

[10] Joshua 3-4

[11] Joshua 14:6-12

[12] Acts 7:21-22

[13] Acts 7:23-24

[14] Acts 7:25-29

[15] Exodus 3:10

[16] Exodus 3:11–4:17. Moses offers four reservations (3:11; 3:13; 4:1; 4:10) which are compellingly answered by God and then finally begs, "Please send someone else." (4:13)

[17] Exodus 7:14–11:10

[18] Exodus 14:13

[19] Exodus 32:1-6

[20] Exodus 32:7-10

[21] Exodus 32:11-14

[22] Numbers 20:2-12

[23] 1 Samuel 20:41-42

[24] 1 Samuel 31:1-3

25 2 Samuel 1:17-27

26 Acts 13:22

27 2 Samuel 11:1-27

28 Psalms 13 and 32 are two powerful examples that will
help you as you become a person after God's heart.

29 2 Samuel 9:1-13

30 Mephibosheth's loyalty to David was questioned by his
servant, Ziba (2 Samuel 16:1-4). David's discernment in
dealing with the confusing situation (2 Samuel 19:24-30)
revealed his discernment.

31 2 Samuel 16:5-12

32 2 Samuel 19:18-23

33 The story of Joseph and his family is found in Genesis 37-
50.

34 Genesis 39:1

35 Genesis 41:38

36 Genesis 42-50. This section of Scripture is full of insights
on sibling relationships.

37 Genesis 50:20

38 Joseph was a man of similar character, though his declara-
tions of future prominence to his brothers (Genesis 37:1-11)
can be seen as a contributing factor in their conflicts.

39 Though we do not know for sure, Isaiah 39:5-7 indicates
that at least some of those taken into Babylon would
become eunuchs (be castrated) as part of their preparation
to serve the king of Babylon. This practice eliminated the
possibility of a servant violating a wife or concubine of the
king.

40 Daniel 1:3-21

41 Daniel 2:1-13

42 Daniel 2:14-23

[43] Daniel 2:28,45

[44] Daniel 2:48

[45] Daniel 4:1-18

[46] Daniel 4:19-27. Notice Daniel's encouragement to the king in verse 27.

[47] Daniel 4:28-33

[48] Daniel 4:34-38

[49] A careful study of Daniel 5-12 will stretch you spiritually and challenge you personally.

[50] A cupbearer was among the most trusted people in a king's court, providing both security and counsel for the king.

[51] Babylon was conquered by Persians in 539 B.C. Zerubbabel led the first group of exiles back to Judah shortly thereafter, with Ezra returning to complete the rebuilding of the temple in 458 B.C. Nehemiah's story begins in 445 B.C.

[52] Nehemiah 1:1-3

[53] Nehemiah 1:4-11

[54] Ephesians 2:8-10

[55] Nehemiah 2:4

[56] James 1:5

[57] Nehemiah 2:1-8

[58] Nehemiah 2:9-10

[59] Nehemiah 2:11-20

[60] Nehemiah 3:1-32. Workers were given responsibilities close to their homes, encouraging both sustained motivation and increased security.

[61] Nehemiah 4:1-6

[62] Nehemiah 4:7-9

[63] Nehemiah 4:10-23

[64] Nehemiah 5:1–6:14. Nehemiah also cared for the poor

while he was rebuilding the walls. Concern for people can be harmonious with finishing challenging tasks.

[65]Philippians 3:4-6

[66] Acts 9:2; 18:25; 19:9; 22:4

[67] Literally decaying food or human excrement

[68] Philippians 3:7-9

[69] Philippians 3:10-11

[70] Philippians 3:12-14

[71] 2 Corinthians 9:15

[72] Acts 2:40-47; 3:4; 4:32-35

[73] Acts 4:36-37

[74] Acts 9:1-19

[75] Acts 9:26-27

[76] Acts 11:19-24

[77] Acts 11:25-26

[78] Acts 13:1-3

[79] Acts 13:4-8

[80] Acts 15:36-41

[81] Acts 13:13

[82] 2 Timothy 4:11

[83] Acts 4:36

GOD'S PLAN

In most athletic contests a coach prepares a game plan ahead of time. God designed a plan for our lives before the world began.

God is holy and perfect. He created us to love Him, glorify Him, and enjoy Him forever.

WHAT IS GOD'S STANDARD?

The Bible, God's playbook, says that the standard for being on His team is to:

Be holy.
"Be holy because I am holy." -1 Peter 1:16

Be perfect.

*"Be perfect, therefore, as your heavenly
Father is perfect."*-Matthew 5:48

WHAT IS GOD'S PLAN?

God created us to:

Love Him.

*"He said to him, 'Love the Lord your God
with all your heart, with all your soul, and
with all your mind.'"*-Matthew 22:37

Glorify (honor) Him.

*"Our Lord and God, You are worthy
to receive glory and honor and power,
because You have created all things,
and because of Your will they exist and
were created."*-Revelation 4:11

Enjoy Him forever.

Jesus said, *"...I have come that they may
have life and have it in abundance."*
                                    -John 10:10

*Why is it that we cannot live up to God's
standard of holiness and perfection and
fulfill God's plan for our lives?
Because of...*

MAN'S PROBLEM

Man is sinful and is separated from God.

WHAT IS SIN?

Sin means missing the mark, falling short
of God's standard. It is not only doing
wrong and failing to do what God wants
(lying, gossip, losing our temper, lustful
thoughts, etc.), but it is also an attitude
of ignoring or rejecting God which is a
result of our sinful nature.

"Indeed, I was guilty [when I] was born..."
                                    -Psalm 51:5

WHO HAS SINNED?

"For all have sinned and fall short of the glory of God."-Romans 3:23

WHAT'S THE RESULT OF SIN?

Separation from God.
"But your iniquities have built barriers between you and your God..."-Isaiah 59:2

Death.
"For the wages of sin is death..."
-Romans 6:23

Judgment.
"...just as it is appointed for people to die once—and after this, judgment"
-Hebrews 9:27

This illustration shows that God is holy and we are sinful and separated from Him. Man continually tries to reach God through his own efforts (being good, religious activities, philosophy, etc.) but, while these can be good things, they all fall short of God's standard.

"All of us have become like something unclean, and all our righteous acts are like a polluted garment..."-Isaiah 64:6

There is only one way to bridge this gap between God and man...

GOD'S SUBSTITUTE

God provided the only way to be on His team by sending His son, Jesus Christ, as the holy and perfect substitute to die in our place.

WHO IS JESUS CHRIST?

He is God.
Jesus said, *"The Father and I are one."*
-John 10:30

He is Man.
"...the Word (Jesus) was God...The Word became flesh and took up residence among us."-John 1:1,14

WHAT HAS JESUS DONE?

He died as our substitute.
"God proves His own love for us in that while we were still sinners Christ died for us!"-Romans 5:8

He rose from the dead.
"...Christ died for our sins..He was buried...He was raised on the third day according to the Scriptures and...He appeared to Cephas, then to the Twelve. Then He appeared to over 500 brothers at one time..."-1 Corinthians 15:3-6

He is the only way to God.
"I am the way, the truth, and the life. No one comes to the Father except through Me."-John 14:6

This diagram shows that God has bridged the gap between Himself and man by sending Jesus Christ to die in our place as our substitute. Jesus defeated sin and death and rose from the grave. Yet, it isn't enough just to know these facts. *The following page tells how to become part of God's team and experience His plan...*

MAN'S RESPONSE

Knowing a lot about a sport and "talking the game" doesn't make you a member of a team. The same is true in becoming a Christian. It takes more than just knowing about Jesus Christ; it requires a total commitment by faith in Him.

FAITH IS NOT:

Just knowing the facts.
"You believe that God is one; you do well. The demons also believe—and they shudder."-James 2:19

Just an emotional experience.
Raising your hand or repeating a prayer
is not enough.

FAITH IS:

Repenting.
Turning to God from sin.
*"For godly grief produces a repentance not
to be regretted and leading to salvation..."*
 -2 Corinthians 7:10

Receiving Jesus Christ.
Trusting in Christ alone for salvation.
*"But to all who did receive Him, He gave
them the right to be children of God, to
those who believe in His name..."*
 -John 1:12

Look at the diagram-
On which side do you see yourself?
Where would you like to be?

Jesus said, *"I assure you: Anyone who
hears My word and believes Him who sent
Me has eternal life and will not come under
judgment but has passed from death to
life."*-John 5:24

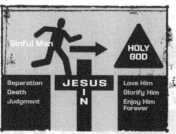

REPLAY OF GOD'S PLAN

 REalize God is holy and perfect; we are
sinners and cannot save ourselves.

 REcognize who Jesus is and what He's
done as our substitute.

 REceive Jesus Christ by faith as Savior
and Lord.
*"But to all who did receive Him, He gave them
the right to become children of God, to those
who believe in His name..."-John 1:12,13*

 REspond to Jesus Christ in a life of
obedience.
*"If anyone wants to come with me, he must
deny himself, take up his cross daily, and
follow Me."-Jesus, Luke 9:23*

Does God's plan make sense to you? Are
you willing to repent and receive Jesus
Christ?

If so, express to God your need for Him.
Consider the "Suggested Prayer of
Commitment" on the next page. Remember
that God is more concerned with your
attitude than with the words you say.

Suggested
PRAYER OF COMMITMENT

"Lord Jesus, I need You. I realize I'm a sinner and I can't save myself. I need Your forgiveness. I believe that You loved me so much that You died on the cross for my sins and rose from the dead. I repent of my sins and put my faith in You as Savior and Lord. Take control of my life and help me to follow You in obedience. I love You Jesus. In Jesus' name. Amen."

"...If you confess with your mouth, 'Jesus is Lord', and believe in your heart that God raised Him from the dead, you will be saved...for 'Everyone who calls on the name of the Lord will be saved.'"
—Romans 10:9,13

Once you have committed your life to Jesus Christ, it is important to understand what your position is on this team...

KNOW YOUR POSITION

Too many people make the mistake of measuring the certainty of their salvation by their feelings instead of the facts of God's Word. In Jesus Christ you have a new life. See what God's Word says about your new position on His team...

N I am a New Creation in Christ.
2 Corinthians 5:17; Galatians 2:20

E I have Everything I need for life and godliness.
2 Peter 1:3; Ephesians 1:3

W I am a Witness for Christ and am His Workmanship, created for good works.
Acts 1:8; Ephesians 2:10

L I am Loved and accepted completely in Christ.
Ephesians 1:6; Romans 8:39

I I am Indwelt by the Holy Spirit.
1 Corinthians 6:19, 20; 1 John 4:4

F I am Forgiven and Free from condemnation.
1 John 1:9; Romans 8:1-2

E I have Eternal Life in Christ.
John 5:24; 1 John 5:11-13

Trust God! Put your faith in His Word, not in your feelings: *"I have written these things to you who believe in the name of the Son of God, so that you may know that you have eternal life."*
—1 John 5:13

4 DAILY EXERCISES

Just as physical growth demands physical exercise, spiritual growth as a Christian demands spiritual exercise. To build spiritual muscle here are four daily exercises.

1. Daily Seek Christ.

Spend time every day reading God's Word and devoting time in prayer.

"...they welcomed the message with eagerness and examined the Scriptures daily to see if these things were so."-Acts 17:11

"I praise You seven times a day..."-Psalm 119:164

2. Daily Share Christ.

Share Jesus every day through your words and actions.

"Every day in the temple complex, and in various homes, they continued teaching and proclaiming the good news that the Messiah is Jesus."
-Acts 5:42

"Therefore, we are ambassadors for Christ; certain that God is appealing through us..."
-2 Corinthians 5:20

3. Daily Lead Others.

Lead others by serving as Christ did. Every day die to self and yield complete control of your life to Jesus Christ.

"The greatest among you will be your servant."
-Matt 23:11

"If anyone wants to come with Me, he must deny himself, take up his cross daily, and follow Me."
-Luke 9:23

4. Daily Love Others.

Take every opportunity to show others around you that you love them.

"...love your neighbor as yourself..."-Mark 12:33

"But encourage each other daily, while it is still called today..."-Heb 3:13

Do these exercises and you will grow strong in your Christian life and be an effective member of God's team.

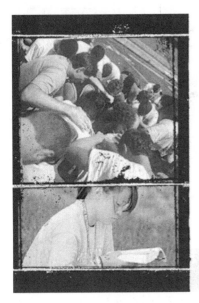

If you made a commitment to Christ, or rededicated your life to Christ, FCA wants to know. Please do one of the following so we can help you:

 1. Log on to www.morethanwinning.org and record your decision.

2. Contact us at 1-800-289-0909 or fca@fca.org.

3. Contact your local FCA office.

FELLOWSHIP OF CHRISTIAN ATHLETES

FCA Vision:
"To see the world impacted for Jesus Christ through the influence of athletes and coaches."

1-800-289-0909
www.fca.org
fca@fca.org

FELLOWSHIP OF CHRISTIAN ATHLETES
8701 Leeds Road
Kansas City, MO 64129

Local Contact Information: